Igniting the Spark

Library Programs That Inspire

Premiere Events: Library Programs That Inspire Elementary School Patrons. By Patricia Potter Wilson and Roger Leslie.

Igniting the Spark: Library Programs That Inspire High School Patrons. By Roger Leslie and Patricia Potter Wilson.

Center Stage: Library Programs That Inspire Middle School Patrons. By Patricia Potter Wilson and Roger Leslie.

Igniting the Spark

Library Programs That Inspire High School Patrons

Roger Leslie
and
Patricia Potter Wilson

2001
Libraries Unlimited
A Division of Greenwood Publishing Group, Inc.
Englewood, Colorado

To my father, who inspires me to dream with courage and work with integrity.
Roger

To Dick Abrahamson, my mentor and friend.
Pat

Libraries Unlimited
A Division of Greenwood Publishing Group, Inc.
P.O. Box 6633
Englewood, CO 80155-6633
www.lu.com

Library of Congress Cataloging-in-Publication Data

Leslie, Roger.
    Igniting the spark : library programs that inspire high school patrons / Roger Leslie and
Patricia Potter Wilson.
       p. cm. -- (Library programs that inspire)
    Includes bibliographical references and index.
    ISBN 1-56308-797-9
     1. High school libraries--Activity programs--United States. 2. Activity programs in
    education--United States. I. Wilson, Patricia J. (Patricia Jane) II. Title.

    Z675.S3 L392 2001
    027.8'223'0973--dc21
                                                                                  2001038431

Contents

List of Illustrations

Figures

Photographs

Acknowledgments

We are grateful to the media specialists, university professors, and friends who supported us throughout this project. First, we thank the 20 school library media specialists who provided the model programs and ideas that make up Chapter 8. That section brings to life every explanation throughout the text. Without their dynamic program ideas, this book could not have been written.

The professors in the School of Education at University of Houston–Clear Lake generously shared their time and knowledge. As always, Ms. Ann Kimzey was there to advise us and proofread the manuscript. Dr. Maureen White encouraged us throughout the project, and her young adult (YA) literature class searched the Internet for interesting Web sites for the YA authors included in Chapter 6. We particularly want to thank Julie Hardegree and Kit Chiu for the numerous hours they spent searching the Internet for outstanding Web sites as well. Finally, this book could never have been completed without the technology skills of Mr. Isidro Grau.

Although many library media specialists were involved in this project, we extend a special thank-you to the University of Houston–Clear Lake students enrolled in school library internships. They worked diligently examining model programs in various school districts. We also thank Dr. Barry Bishop and Ms. Diane Durbin for their support throughout the project.

Finally, we thank Jerry Roberts, Wendell Wilson, and Richard and Jerry Leslie for sharing our vision and enthusiasm for this book.

Introduction

On an ordinary work day several years ago, I changed my vision of what my school library media center should be. During first period, I began helping a class choose fiction for book reports. The reading teacher had only one selection criterion: The book had to contain at least 100 pages. To my frustration, it was the only criterion that the students used as well.

"What do you like?" I asked. "Adventure? Love stories? Horror?"

"Mr. Leslie, I hate to read, so I don't care," nearly every student replied. "Just make it 100 pages."

I had witnessed this lack of interest evolve over many years and had even inadvertently contributed to what was becoming an epidemic problem. To meet student needs, I perused catalogs and reference materials such as Joni Richards Bodart's *The World's Best Thin Books* to order easy reading, high interest titles. Books by Avi, Jay Bennett, and Gary Paulsen, all excellent writers for middle school students, were squeezing out authors like Alice Walker and Walter Dean Myers, not to mention the greats whose classics now served only as dust mite headquarters worthy of a science experiment.

When I was an English teacher, I had successfully introduced seniors to Chekov, Kafka, even Joyce. As a school library media specialist trying to meet the needs of all grade levels, I watched my educational ideals fade under a desperate attempt to pull students into the library media center however I could. When studying my periodical circulation records that fateful day, I grew heartsick. Ninety percent of all magazine requests were for *Low Rider* and *WWF,* titles I initially refused to add to my collection.

Although these magazines may be both entertaining and useful in some contexts, the power they had wielded in my high school library media center embarrassed me. Instead of broadening the scope of my resources, I had merely lowered my expectations of what students could handle or even cared to attempt. It was a destructive cycle that I was determined to stop.

Originally, I had no greater vision for changing my professional focus than to make my facility more meaningful to patrons. But when Patricia Potter Wilson and I agreed to write a series of books on library programming, I realized that my own experience was the springboard for this second installment of the series.

The first work, *Premiere Events: Library Programs that Inspire Elementary School Patrons*, formed a natural blend of topic and audience: Programs can comprise the very core of elementary curriculum. But for the secondary level, I had concerns. Programs can be any activities, great or small, that support learning and encourage patrons to use the school library media center. However, like many of my contemporaries, I once perceived them as rare, sometimes unworkable additions to my daily responsibilities. I was wrong. As my co-author and I learned when surveying high school library media specialists throughout the country, and as we hope you will discover from their contributions to this book, library programs are not infrequent events that drain already overextended media specialists. Instead, just as they do at the elementary level, library programs invigorate, expand, and enrich the school library media center's role in education. Just as important, they often distinguish the most successful specialists at award-winning high schools (many of whom contributed program ideas to this text) from media specialists slowly burning out from the new responsibilities that global education has demanded of us all.

Library programming is as integral to the profession as circulation, research, and administration. Surprisingly, however, between Patricia Potter Wilson's *Happenings: Developing Successful Programs for School Libraries*, and our first book in this series, very few publications have even addressed the topic exclusively. At best, as in the case of Carolyn Feller Bauer's resources on programming with children's literature and Joni Bodart's *Booktalk* series, it was generally covered in a larger context.

Then Libraries Unlimited suggested that we write a series of books on this topic, long in need of representation on our professional shelves. Although my co-author and I share a career background as school library media specialists, our unique contributions to the work come from diverse experiences in the field. Patricia Potter Wilson was an elementary school teacher and library media specialist before earning her doctorate in education. As a university professor who teaches school library science courses, she emphasizes program development in her curriculum, even adding a programming component to the school library administration course as well as to the internship. In addition to her research on professional collections, she is also nationally recognized for her efforts to add a school library component to all graduate programs for aspiring school principals.

As a lifelong educator, I have had much first-hand experience seeing what motivates students to learn. Besides helping me develop programming in my secondary school library media center, that knowledge has inspired my novels and nonfiction works, including my forthcoming motivational book for teens, *Train of Dreams*. Further, being a YA book reviewer for *Booklist* has provided first-hand knowledge of resource topics of interest to teen patrons and has kept me apprised of publishing trends.

For this book, we have three objectives: 1) to offer detailed information for planning, executing, and assessing school library programs; 2) to emphasize the benefits of such programs; and 3) to share winning program ideas developed and carried out by high school media specialists at award-winning schools across the nation. (Chapter 8 describes their programs in detail.) We also incorporate numerous program ideas throughout the text. When sharing original suggestions submitted by only one professional, we credit that person by name. When including identical or overlapping ideas from more than one school library media specialist, we combine them for clarity and use a generic name or description.

We sincerely believe that programming is one of the most powerful tools for any media specialist. Its benefits are vast and long lasting. Programming promotes lifelong reading and learning. It supports and enriches curriculum. It can encourage consistent, loyal patronage by students and faculty. Perhaps most important, it advertises and promotes the school library media center, making an impression on the student body, your colleagues, and the entire community of which your facility is an integral part. By suggesting topics, leading you to appropriate resources, and explaining the step-by-step process of executing program plans, we hope to inspire you to create programs.

Chapter by Chapter Preview

Using an example from my own experience, **Chapter 1** introduces a model program that we trace, stage-by-stage, throughout the text. Following this example we offer an extensive working definition of library programming, both determining exactly what constitutes a program and distinguishing the term *library program* in this context from its generic reference to all duties required of media specialists.

Chapter 2 describes several options for planning a library program. Because these initial steps support all subsequent stages, good planning is paramount to the success of a program. Beyond traditional methods of determining student interest and selecting a theme, we also share unique ideas from several library media specialists that enhance the process.

Chapter 3 explains effective ways to gather and organize programming information. Whether your program is a simple interactive display or an elaborate, week-long event, careful planning and meticulous organization ensure the greatest benefits for audiences and the least frustration for you.

After completing initial program planning, you need access to the most useful information, resources, and support staff available. **Chapter 4** shares surprising suggestions for accessing hard-to-find resources, and **Chapter 5** provides dynamic strategies for recruiting and instructing volunteers.

The global focus on our profession has created some often overwhelming responsibilities. But with them has come access to information as we have never seen before. Consequently, **Chapter 6** offers a list of some of the best Internet sites related to school subjects and topics of interest to young adults.

As with any project, assessment and evaluation are essential for determining what worked effectively and what needs revision. **Chapter 7** recommends numerous assessment tools and sample evaluations for illuminating your program strengths and weaknesses. Perhaps even more helpful are the subsequent suggestions for enhancing good programs that you may want to repeat, refining good ideas that initially did not result in a strong program or eliminating programs that no longer meet student needs.

Chapter 8 opens the creative floodgates with outstanding sample programs from library media specialists throughout the United States. Covering an array of topics across the curriculum, these innovative, entertaining, and effective programs showcase colleagues at the height of their creativity. You may host these same programs on your campus or tailor the details to the precise needs of your school population.

Throughout the book we aspire to do more than merely generate interest in library programming. Rather, we hope to supply you with tools for reaching more high school students and affecting them more deeply than you have before. No one in our profession needs more work. However, we could use a new vision for igniting the spark of interest in students who may have a background of resistance to reading or negative stereotypes about the media center and the people who run it. Although no single philosophy will magically enhance an entire profession, the new vision we espouse can certainly inspire the creativity just waiting to be stirred in you, as well as the potential ready to be tapped in students.

Chapter 1

Igniting the Spark for You and Your Patrons

When I accepted the media specialist position at the school where I taught, I replaced a diligent professional who, like most of us, revered books.

"She protected them like children," my secretary told me. "And she wouldn't part with one."

As it turned out, there was much that my predecessor had held onto. Unfortunately, the school first opened in the 1930s, and the inventory grew well beyond the facility that housed it. My first week on the job, I set out to rid the school library media center of clutter. I organized drawers, rearranged the periodical room, and prepared the main lobby for patrons. With teachers still attending inservice at another campus, I came to work in my oldest jeans and T-shirt and tackled the biggest project of all, cleaning out the equipment and storage rooms. I could barely wend my way through them without tripping over either pieces of equipment only Ben Franklin would know how to use or resources with dust thicker than his wig.

I suddenly became "Library Man," fighting the crime of outdated information and useless equipment and making my media center safe for learning. To my surprise, this jungle of junk turned out to be much like my grandmother's attic. Instead of filling trash bins and creating heaps for the district maintenance crew to dispose of, I found a slice of history that teachers would love. My first library program, and the philosophy that changed my professional role, was already taking shape.

I had heard little about library programming in my college course work. On the rare occasions when it was mentioned at all, I usually dismissed the information as applicable only to elementary school media specialists. In my children's literature course, I had fun constructing displays and manipulatives for a center. But in the end, I gave all those materials to my group partners. After all, I would be a high school media specialist. I wouldn't be doing any such activities.

I was wrong. Sharing the stored materials in my school library media center led to my first program. More important, it tipped me off to what ignited a spark in patrons that brought them into the school library media center and inspired them to return. By the time I had completed only a handful of programs, I realized that they were not extraneous events that I might add to the already overwhelming responsibilities of my job. Instead, they were vibrant, sometimes ongoing, occasionally overlapping activities that generated interest in learning and promoted my school library media center.

My first library event excited teachers so much, I thought Maria Montessori or Madeline Hunter would call and invite me into some exclusive club for innovators in education. In truth, I was only doing my job. But the creative approach invigorated me, excited my patrons, and made programs a core element of my work.

I called my first event "The Great Book Giveaway." To get teachers interested, I intentionally played up the idea of offering something for free. It worked. After weeding all the irrelevant resources and disposing of useless equipment, I still had many duplicate copies of noncirculating books and extra pieces of equipment for which I didn't have enough storage space. Thus, to make room in my media center for new resources, I determined to give old materials to teachers for classroom use.

My first program advertisement was simple. I informed teachers that the school library media center had books, games, kits, video- and audiotapes, record albums (yes, really), film strips, and even some old carts and equipment to give away on a first-come, first-served basis. The doors would open at 7:00 a.m., and there was no limit to what anyone could have. I made this offer in part to let teachers have what they needed. In truth, however, I mostly wanted to pique teacher interest so that I could replace outdated resources. Although the materials I gave away were no longer effective for library research, they all contained something—a diagram, activities, historical data—that would serve as a useful supplement in a classroom.

I made only one request of anyone who attended the giveaway. Every visitor had to take three sheets of paper I had prepared for the event. The first shared general information about the procedures and resources currently available in the school library media center. The second listed new materials I had recently ordered. The third requested input from teachers concerning resources they wanted me to add to the collection.

The day before the event, teachers who passed the school library media center saw me arranging the weeded items into attractive displays. News spread throughout campus. By the end of the day, teachers were asking if they could claim items in advance.

"We're open at 7:00," I'd smile. "Whoever gets here first can have it."

I arrived at 6:30 the next morning. Teachers were already lined up outside my door. Some brought grocery bags or small boxes to carry away their goods. One science teacher, among the first in line, had a trash compactor box on a dolly, ready to haul off his take. I was astounded.

When I opened the doors, teachers raced around my display tables like a rerun of *Supermarket Sweep*. Clearly, my library junk was their classroom treasure. I had hoped to rid my library of all these excess materials by the end of the day. Before the first period bell rang at 7:20, nearly every table was cleared. Except for a few pamphlets and paperback novels that I later donated to the chairperson of the English department, there was nothing left but dust from the race and a few skid marks from the science teacher's dolly. After the whirlwind event, I pondered what made it such a surprising hit and wondered how I might translate this type of activity into a valuable learning experience for students.

Besides providing my first success as a media specialist, this isolated event taught me something about patrons that I never needed to know as a teacher. In the library media center, I had to find innovative ways to get students through the door. In the classroom, I used several techniques to keep students engaged. Now, I had a new challenge: How do I get students who generally don't like to read or who hold negative stereotypes about libraries to enter in the first place? The answer is library programming.

Media Center Programming Defined

The event described above includes the central ingredient necessary for a library program: a learning objective. Although the book giveaway brought in teachers and moved out clutter, my learning component appeared on the information sheets. They let teachers know what was available and invited them to participate in acquiring new resources.

Like any good lesson, school library media programs should be so engaging that learning occurs seamlessly. Had I simply invited teachers in for some coffee and a quick tour of the facility, attendance would likely have been dismal. If I placed the sheets in teachers' mailboxes, most would not have gotten much farther than the recycle bin. Creating a media center event took me through many of the stages and benefits of a well-executed program: planning, promotion, organization, and assessment.

In general, a school library media center program is any special event consisting of planned activities that are developed and shared to achieve predetermined learning objectives. This broad definition allows for flexibility in every stage of programming. Depending on your inventiveness and interest, you may choose from numerous topics, formats, resources, schedules, and audiences that best meet your learning objectives. The resulting program may range from simple displays or single speaker presentations to elaborate, week-long events open to the school population and the community.

In any form, media center programs are created to serve the needs of students and faculty. Done well, they simultaneously engender a positive perception of school library media centers, encourage patrons to frequent the media center more often, and increase the use and circulation of resources. Media specialists usually call the entire body of work responsibilities their "school library media center program." Throughout this text the words "program" and "programming" refer exclusively to special events that fulfill specific learning objectives; increase school library media center use; and enhance the reputation of the facility within the school, district, and community.

Types of Programs

Although library media center responsibilities are often repetitive, programming is flexible and creative. Even media specialists who contributed model programs to this book were surprised to discover how many activities actually constituted programs. Like lesson plans, programs require three components: a clear learning objective, a plan for presenting information, and assessment strategies to gauge the lesson's effectiveness. But unlike lesson plans, which are often developed by grade level committees and restricted to a set curriculum established by the state or district, library programs are usually original creations of the media specialist. From their simplest to their most elaborate forms, library programs are flexible teaching strategies that can often be created, modified, or eliminated at the sole discretion of the media specialist.

Exhibits and Displays

School library media centers frequently contain simple displays or even multifaceted exhibits. A freestanding book display placed beneath an eye-catching bulletin board is perhaps the most common type of program. Whether changed monthly, seasonally, or only when new books arrive, a simple display piques interest and personalizes the atmosphere of the school library media center. Displays can become elaborate expressions of your creativity. From three-dimensional wall decorations to interactive bulletin boards, displays are learning tools that intrigue young patrons.

Photo 1.1. Dazzling displays like this holiday showcase at Menchville High School in Newport News, Virginia, attract patrons to the library media center.

Library media specialists, teachers, or students can construct effective exhibits. If your budget allows, you may also rent or purchase them from sources beyond the campus. (Some of those sources are mentioned in Chapter 4.) Exhibits can enhance guest speakers' presentations or reinforce a research topic. Often, teachers ask to display student projects in the school library media center after a unit, competition, or fair. Alone, such exhibits are mere decorations, but add a learning component such as a fact sheet or interactive quiz or game, and they become programs. Arranging topic-related library books near the exhibit is the easiest way to add a library learning element. Yet more effective possibilities are also available. Offering tip sheets for online databases (see Figure 1.1) or a list of Internet sites under the heading "For Further Reading" gives curious students an accessible guide to continue their learning.

TELL ME ABOUT PROQUEST DIRECT

U.M.I. PROQUEST DIRECT is an Internet site that features abstracts and indexes of articles from over 140 of the best U.S. news magazines and general reference publications, plus *The New York Times* and *USA Today*. Full-text articles are provided for more than 100 publications. Each entry contains a complete bibliographic citation, followed by either an abstract or the entire text of the article.

Special Features

- A "HOW TO" menu takes you step-by-step through the search process.
- Related subject headings listed beside each article citation expand search possibilities.
- Examples of search strategies appear with both search method options.
- Full-text articles and abstracts can be printed.
- A help menu can be accessed by pressing the F1 key at any screen during the research process.
- Sample bibliographical citations are provided in both MLA and APA formats.

Figure 1.1. Sample tip sheet for electronic databases.

Arrange valuable display and exhibit materials in a locked case. Occasionally, artifacts or mementos shared by teachers or rented from local museums bring topics to life more vividly than photographs and handouts. Although protected, materials may be left out longer or rearranged and added to for long-term interest.

Featured Speakers and Entertainers

Elementary and middle school media specialists frequently invite guest presenters to share information or skills with students. Throughout the year, visiting authors, puppeteers, or storytellers captivate young audiences. However, rigorous curriculum demands and strict scheduling requirements often prevent high school students from attending such entertaining events. Programs centering around guest speakers are often the most effective teaching tools available to library media specialists. Instead of requiring students to look in reference books for information on Vietnam, for example, invite a veteran of the war to speak about personal experiences. Rather than giving booktalks on several new resources about drug abuse and addiction, ask an emergency room nurse or drug rehabilitation counselor to recount stories and answer questions for a target audience. As support, provide handouts (your speaker may supply them) and have resources on the topic available for student checkout.

School-wide career days, college recruitment seminars, and multicultural fairs are common annual events in high schools. But guest speakers who share personal information relating to core curriculum, electives, or general interest add unique, sometimes rare dimensions to the learning environment.

Interest Centers

Once used primarily by elementary school teachers, interest centers are now being used by media specialists. From simple centers arranged on tables or study carrels to elaborate partitioned areas that can accommodate several small groups simultaneously, interest centers invite interactive learning that students pursue at their own pace.

Interest centers may begin small and grow over time. One library media specialist developed an interest center by displaying history books, maps, and flags around Civil War trivia cards. Over time, the collection and a game evolved. The media specialist displayed, in a locked case, authentic Civil War memorabilia including letters, photographs, caps, boots, and eventually a scale model battle scene created by one teacher's U. S. history classes. The following year that same teacher challenged her students to create a Civil War board game. For a while, the game (a combination of Stratego and Trivial Pursuit) became so popular that the history club held a tournament in the media center.

Demonstrations

Demonstrations make successful programs because they encourage interaction between students and the media specialist, teacher, or guest facilitator. Instead of giving an oral presentation, the facilitator demonstrates a process. Whether baking a dessert, creating a Web site, or role playing a successful job interview, demonstrations allow students to watch, respond to, and practice real-life experiences. Demonstrations work as part of a large, multifaceted program with centers and displays or as independent activities. In either context, they appeal to curious, energetic students, especially kinesthetic learners.

Media

As libraries became school library media centers, media solidly formed a cornerstone of our profession. Not surprisingly, then, media programs are now among the most popular and relevant programs in high school. Videos, recordings, and multimedia presentations can be the exclusive means for sharing information. Also, media can serve as both the primary teaching tool and the program topic. For example, you may help students create PowerPoint presentations or teach faculty how to navigate a new research database. Because teachers need to master computer skills and many students require fast-paced, multi-image formats to keep their attention, media programs are relevant.

Photo 1.2. Media can comprise both the format and content of programs, like this introduction to electronic catalog searches at Michigan's Byron Center High School.

Programming Foundations

Writing a mission statement clarifies the goals of a business or campus. Similarly, selecting a focus for your program cements the foundation upon which it can be built. Knowing your focus (your program purpose), you can build your program to meet the learning objectives for your target audience.

Programs Based on Curriculum

Very often, school library media specialists select program topics based on curricular needs. Whether offered to develop research skills or to teach learning objectives for a particular subject area, programs based on curriculum are among the most flexible and meaningful. Unlike your elementary school colleagues, you are probably not required to teach daily library classes. Consequently, you are freer to develop programs based on student needs and interests as they arise. Much like the proverbial "teachable moment," simple programs created to meet the immediate needs of students can be riveting and relevant.

Elaborate programs built around curriculum can also be versatile. They allow you to vary your activities and repeat programs year after year. As any teacher knows, the same approach does not necessarily inspire different classes in the same way. Consequently, you may want to modify larger programs over the years to meet the needs of new groups and to enrich and supplement curriculum. Also, because curriculum demands continue to change, you will always have new inspirations for developing programs that correspond to classroom learning.

Programs Based on Target Groups

Another way to select a program topic is to target a specific audience. Groups from the smallest advanced placement classes to entire grade levels can serve as inspiration for program development. Because many skills apply to a vast cross-section of the student population, choosing a target group allows you to customize programs to the exact learning needs of that group.

You are free to target any size or type of audience. Different ages, subject areas, and extracurricular groups are obvious choices. But just as relevant, and sometimes even more inspiring, are program ideas designed for more unique groups. For example, some library media specialists select as their first specialized target group their most frequent patrons, students who read for escape and who seek isolation in the school library media center because they are either new to a school or lack the social skills to immediately find a network of peers with whom to interact. After reading about the Columbine tragedy, one school library media specialist in Michigan helped reclusive students feel valued. His target audience wasn't difficult to identify: These students waited outside his school library media center every morning as he arrived, checked out books, then sat and read nearly every lunch hour, and waited alone for rides after school whenever they missed their bus.

Naturally, his program focus was reading. With his target group in mind, he created a program that taught writing and computer skills while allowing students to interact with peers. Under the guise of needing help sharing new resources, he developed a program to teach students how to review books. Program participants formed a book review team. After the training, students chose books, then wrote brief reviews. Once they completed their work, team members chose some for publication in the school library media center newsletters and others for posting on the school's Web page. Gradually, the group grew, and each member became a better writer, critical reader, and print and Internet publisher. More consistent with the program's purpose, the students developed friendships.

Of course, target groups do not have to be this specialized, and the programs need not be ongoing. Target audiences might be specific classes, entire grade levels, or certain populations (such as gifted and talented or special education students). Whoever the program audience is, contour your topic to their educational or personal development needs.

Programs Based on Special Themes

Because their parameters are so specific, programs based on special themes are often the easiest to develop. Educational needs of a target audience, school- or district-wide events (such as science fairs or multicultural celebrations), or community festivals may determine program themes. Most often, themes correlate with curriculum, personal interests of the media specialist or students, or a combination of these. Not long after attending a lecture by *Titanic* explorer Robert Ballard, school library media specialist Rose Bell was helping an English class do literary analysis of *Lord of the Flies*. Deciding to combine required curriculum with her own passion for the *Titanic* story, she developed a special program on survival for all freshman English students. Scheduling it for the day of the campus blood drive, she invited a Red Cross volunteer to teach CPR, team-taught a first aid session with the school nurse, and even recruited student athletic trainers to assist.

To supplement the information, Rose shared brief booktalks on nonfiction books, including Ballard's *Lost Liners: From the Titanic to the Andrea Doria* (of which she'd purchased several signed copies at Ballard's lecture), as well as novels ranging in reading level from *Hatchet* to *Robinson Crusoe*. Although sparked by her own love of *Titanic* lore, she used the thematic approach to offer students a rich and meaningful learning experience. Examples of other themes that encompass many facets include the immigrant experience (language, custom, travel, health, genealogy) and humor (pop culture, history, creative writing, comic book art, political satire). Almost any hobby, topic, or avocation can serve as the springboard for a theme appropriate for student learning.

Programs Based on Interest and Entertainment

Although you can base a thematic program on your own expertise, it may be easier and more meaningful for students if you develop programs around their interests. With entertainment as a major objective, media specialists often have their most captive audiences at programs exploring topics that students love. Noticing what students read about or search on the Internet during their free time can provide the perfect clues to what students want to learn. From Oscar de la Hoya, to modeling careers, to innovative ways to earn money, there are no limits to topics based on student interest.

Beverly Jones, a school library media specialist and senior class sponsor, hosted a program in the gym for seniors anticipating the prom. At first such a program would hardly seem rife with educational potential. Yet Jones was able to fulfill her duties both as a media specialist and prom committee chairperson by hosting a resoundingly successful event.

She included the local businesses (formal wear shops, florists, disc jockeys, and limousine services) who'd been selected by the prom committee as potential clients, as well as dance instructors and even drug and drinking awareness groups that promote safe, alcohol-free and drug-free celebration. While simultaneously offering useful services to her audience in a context relevant to students, she also inspired much learning. Thanks to the help of the vocational staff, Beverly helped students assess the aforementioned businesses that pitched their product or service. Although vendors' presentations were an integral part of the program presentation, their greatest value was as a springboard for the subsequent assessment. Using the vendors' presentations as her forum, a vocational counselor taught a lesson on consumer awareness.

Collaborating with the drill team coach, Beverly scheduled simultaneous dance instruction sessions led by drill team officers. (Their contribution to the program fulfilled part of their final exam requirements.) Pamphlets from a nearby drug counseling center and from the campus S.A.D.D. (Students Against Driving Drunk) sponsor supplemented book resources from her own school library media center. All stressed the importance of responsible decision making in social situations.

In her program, Jones combined two professional roles, library media specialist and senior class sponsor, to put on an event that supported vocational curriculum, used reading resources, and had real meaning for her target audience. Throughout, students were eager to participate because they wanted a memorable prom. Most impressively, Jones took an event that always distracted seniors during school and usually overwhelmed the handful of class leaders and transformed it into a multifaceted educational experience for all participants.

Programs Based on Time

Sample programs shared in previous categories were elaborate and extensive. However, not every program is meant to be an extravaganza. Often, the complexity and sophistication of a program depend on many different factors.

One essential consideration for all library media specialists is time. As you begin to incorporate programming into your routine, consider the amount of time available for preparing, executing, and assessing any program. Your time is valuable and, like most people in education, already limited by countless responsibilities. Consequently, you may use time as the basis for developing programs.

Like every other type of program, of course, the boundaries for time-dictated programs are limitless. Media specialists who use programming as the framework for their entire profession take whole grading periods to host evolving, expanding, and diverse programs. Others may decide to create a one-time, 30-minute program to teach a specific skill to a single class, or re-teach an idea to a group who clearly did not demonstrate mastery during their last visit to the media center. Exhibits or displays can be especially time effective. Often, you can assemble them quickly, especially if you have help from another professional, support personnel, or volunteers. Best of all, exhibits and displays can be used for any length of time, from a single day to an entire year.

Frequently, short-term programs that involve guest speakers become routine events that students anticipate with excitement. For ongoing or regularly repeated programs, less and less preparation time is required. Additionally, assessments can be honed and completed more expeditiously.

When basing your program decisions on time, also consider the timeliness of a program topic. Some media specialists create programs based on specific holidays or events that occur at certain times of the year. Special events that spur program ideas may be annual, such as the Super Bowl or the announcing of Nobel Prize winners, or they may occur at regular intervals, like the Olympics. One media specialist allows the senior counselor to prepare students for annual scholarships with special computerized resources housed in the school library media center. Using these resource tools, students research scholarship options on the Internet. On one Saturday each autumn, seniors, graduating juniors, and their parents are invited to attend a program about filling out scholarship applications and writing winning scholarship essays.

Without doubt, there are many types of programs and flexible ways to inspire patrons. Once you determine some purposes for your program, choosing program types and formats becomes clear.

Purposes of Programs

Fulfilling learning objectives is the purpose of all programming. Once you have established that purpose, creative ideas for the program type and format abound.

Support and Enhance the Curriculum

One constant in education is emphasis on core curricula. Theoretically, students develop their primary thinking skills by mastering the four major subject areas: language arts, social studies, math, and science. At the secondary level, learning is either rounded out or specialized with electives in ever-growing disciplines.

Although this standard has remained a constant throughout most of the last century, shifts in education during the 1980s and 1990s have opened new opportunities for school library media specialists. Twenty years ago, public school teachers had much more freedom to personalize their lessons to meet particular needs of students or enhance their own unique strengths as instructors. With ever-increasing emphasis placed on standardized tests to determine student success, the curriculum has all but become the tests. As a result, many teachers are also restricted to sharing only prewritten lessons that they didn't create. In many districts across the country, entire teams of teachers are facing the disheartening, even stifling requirement of teaching the same lessons the same way on the same day.

Fortunately, such limitations are seldom as strictly enforced in school library media centers. Through programming, you can develop original lessons that support and enhance the curriculum with a flexibility of format, time, and approach seldom afforded today's teachers.

Both required and elective courses outside the four core curriculum areas also allow library media specialists to employ innovative approaches to learning. From speech and journalism, to drama and choir, to metal trades and computer programming, the course offerings of any school are a cornucopia of program possibilities.

English/Language Arts Curriculum

Not surprisingly, many school library media specialists are former reading, English, or language arts teachers. It is no wonder, then, that English instructors and library media specialists share a close bond. More often than not, they were immersed in collaborative teaching long before the concept became an educational standard. English teachers naturally gravitate to school library media specialists for research material, resources, and suggestions for either those students required to read independently or those exceptional students who enjoy recreational reading.

Your love of books, passion for the written word, and abundant access to information are a wellspring of programming ideas. Among the most effective forms of programming for English/language arts are author visits. Although these are common at the elementary level, fewer high school media specialists invite authors eager to visit schools and share their work with young adults. Works by writers such as Rob Thomas, Joan Lowry Nixon, and Randy Powell resonate with teen readers. Imagine the impact of having such writers visit a campus to share their work, writing techniques, or careers with a target audience. (See the "Young Adult Author Biographies" section in Chapter 6.)

Frequently, author visits are more costly than other types of programs. Yet high school library media specialists have advantages that elementary level specialists do not. Because their campus and student populations are usually much larger, so is their budget. Although yearly author visits may not be financially feasible, part of a book, travel, or contracted services budget could be reserved or transferred in anticipation of just such an event.

Like elementary schools, secondary campuses can also pool resources to share the cost and benefits of an author visit. With the current push toward interlibrary loan, what better way to share resources than to also share a visit? For districts with more than one high school, multiple campuses can gather at one location or arrange for the author to spend part of the day at each site. Seemingly exorbitant fees become manageable when you divide expenses and note the benefits to students. Sometimes, costs can be shared between your school library media center and local bookstores. Also consider inviting authors who are scheduled to speak at conferences in your city. For many authors, their fee includes the price of their airfare and hotel. If a local organization is already paying those expenses, your cost may be lessened considerably.

Do not dismiss the possibility of securing authors who charge little or even nothing but the chance to sell their books. Speaking engagements by lesser known writers are often affordable. Eager to establish a positive reputation, newly published authors frequently work hard to ensure that their visit is a success.

Other English programs require little expense and no outside guest speakers. High school students enjoy some of the same activities frequently used at the elementary level, as long as the program is designed to meet their interests and needs. Booktalks, read alouds, and even storytelling can be very effective for the right group and topic. For many years, students in my school wanted to research rap music, to no avail. I could never find good book resources, and all Internet sites were blocked. Over time, however, I amassed articles from newspapers, magazines, *Current Biography*, and news databases about the music industry and the deaths of some famous rappers. More recently, I began finding books on hip hop and even some well-written articles in new reference materials about contemporary music, such as the three-volume set, *Your Parents Aren't Supposed to Like It.*

To advertise the availability of new resources on the topic, I invited interested students to read aloud not only published tributes to their favorite rappers but also some of their own original poetry. To recruit volunteer readers and invite participants, I made announcements over the school intercom and created simple signs that I hung at the entrance to the school library media center and down the main school corridor. Prior to the event, students signed up to read either biographical sketches that I provided from library resources or original poems, copies of which they submitted for my approval beforehand. For the event, which took place during the lunch periods of one school week, three or four students read for approximately five minutes each. With approval from the administration and after my personal preview, some students performed their poems as raps with accompanying background music.

In general, poetry readings are surprisingly popular, especially when interspersing original poems written by students with classic and contemporary verse by famous writers. At one school, the library media specialist hosts a tribute to women in history that includes lunch time poetry reading sessions. Students sign up to hear volunteer teachers and students read contemporary poetry written by famous women and by their peers. In some years, the library media specialist focuses on specific artists and themes, like Nikki Giovanni and love, or even specific poetry collections, such as *Leaving Yuba City* by Chitra Banerjee Divakaruni. In other years she concentrates on a type of poem or literary period, allowing students to create works to fit the style or genre.

During National Library Week, a colleague in my district has teachers read excerpts from their favorite books to students during lunch. Not surprisingly, the variety is astounding. In one lunch period, students might hear *The Great Gatsby, Tuesdays with Morrie, Math Curse,* and *Chicken Soup for the Teenage Soul II.* On the last day, she invites teachers who have published poetry or prose to read from their original works, then answer questions about writing and publishing. For that session, she sends special invitations to the creative writing classes encouraging them to attend.

Because creating lifelong readers is a primary objective of all media specialists, English programs are the most frequently developed. More examples, and further details on programs like those described here, appear in Chapter 8.

Social Studies Curriculum

Because of its diversity, social studies curriculum affords countless programming opportunities. Multicultural studies have become the cornerstone of teaching tolerance and diversity in schools throughout the country. As the core of any school, the library media center is the ideal place to offer exciting programs during multicultural week. In many cases, entire campuses host school-wide multicultural fairs in which every department is required to participate. During that week, visitors might see paper dragons cascading over the science wing during a tae kwon do demonstration, catch a whiff of tortillas wafting through the history hallway, and hear bagpipes blaring from the girls' gym.

Although no one person, not even the library media specialist, should be expected to coordinate an entire festival, you will want to be on the planning committee. If nothing else, volunteer the media center as a hub of activity. For example, it could serve as a mock United Nations drawing together different cultures being taught throughout the building.

Social studies curriculum allows for hosting smaller programs as well. To incorporate geography information and help students learn about their teachers at the beginning of the year, school library media specialist Kelly Schultz posts a huge map on a bulletin board that identifies where all the teachers traveled the previous summer. Different colored yarn traces the distance from school to each destination. Over the years, her single map has evolved into an entire display. Not only did this concept inspire more teachers to share their travel exploits, but it also prompted a faculty tradition of sending souvenir postcards to Kelly and occasionally bringing her artifacts unique to various regions.

Historical periods or events can also prompt programming ideas. One teacher's annual field trip to the Holocaust Museum in Houston inspired library media specialist Dean Glen to offer a program on World War II. Because his school is located in a community with many seniors, he gathered first-hand accounts of being in the war or waiting for loved ones back home from people in his town. Eventually, his "My War" event included information about soldiers and key battles, biographical information about major historical figures, and, best of all, copies of actual letters from loved ones who had corresponded during the war. These personalized accounts were displayed with books like *Thanks to My Mother* by Schoschana Ravinovici and Elie Wiesel's *Night*, copies of which were available for checkout from the school library media center as well as from the classroom collection. Like many institutions, the Holocaust Museum had many relevant resources and special displays available for just such units.

Through programming, you can support the social studies curriculum in ways limited only by your enthusiasm. From simple bulletin boards to events that become the common thread for an entire district-wide fair, programs on social issues, geography, government, or history can be fascinating learning experiences.

Science Curriculum

Because it may have the most display area in the entire school, the library media center often becomes the host facility for building-level science fair competitions. However, you can do much more than close the library for a day or stay late a few evenings to give the judges an opportunity to select the best projects. Instead, you can incorporate their unique contributions to the event, provide extended learning for classes, and honor students who made exceptional projects.

Best of all, with a little ingenuity, you can keep student contributions simple. Just this year, the science department at my school reserved the library media center to display poster and tri-fold projects to be judged by a panel of teachers. Although the projects were arranged randomly, I recognized recurring themes in projects throughout the room, including some on the planting, gestation, and fertilizing of common grasses. When the competition was completed, I arranged for the students who did those projects to leave their displays in the library media center and worked with an earth science teacher to offer a program to her class.

Combining our budgets, she and I bought one small plant for each student who would attend the program. I then strategically arranged them, unlabeled, throughout the school library media center based on the amount of light each plant needed to grow. At the circulation desk, I gathered some resources on plant life and gardening but left some on the shelves for students to find on their own as well.

During the program, the three science fair contestants described their experiments. Afterward, the teacher gave a lesson on caring for plant life, pointing out the resources I had gathered to help students with the assignment that would conclude the program. Each student was to select one of the plants and become its caretaker for the rest of the semester. As the plants grew, students were to identify the plant, then complete a questionnaire about it relating everything from how much sunlight and water it needed to where such plants flourished and what uses (for example, food, medicine) the plant served.

Naturally, students had to read some of the resources to complete the assignment and had to frequent the school library center regularly to care for their plants. The blooming plants added esthetically to the facility, and of course, patronage increased markedly because students were being graded for their work.

Thus, any school activity can spark a program idea. For years, I felt frustrated when the science department interrupted research schedules by taking over my facility for a day. With a little ingenuity, the science teacher and I created a win/win situation. Together, we enabled some students to share their projects, developed a lesson that the teacher didn't have room to execute in her classroom, and increased usage of the library media center.

Math Curriculum

For many years, bookshelves for math resources were too often sparse and in desperate need of updating. Although new books about math may still be harder to come by than those in other core curricula, the advent of computers and a burgeoning interest in high tech career research has opened the floodgate for programs that incorporate math concepts.

Very often, math programs can be offered in conjunction with some other discipline. Math classes surfing the Internet for examples of fractals in nature led one media specialist to combine science and math for a program on the topic. The media specialist and the math instructor offered a mini-lesson, hosted in the science lab, that included microscopic examinations of fractals in leaves and ice shavings. A simple bibliography of book resources available in the school library media center and a Webography of worthwhile sites found by previous classes extended the learning.

Combining core curriculum with community service, another library media specialist helped a geometry instructor give a real-world lesson on tesselation, the consistent patterning of polygons. During the planning stages of some school renovations, both educators secured permission to have a class assist in the design of a small courtyard area. As the library media specialist gathered information and examples from library books and landscaping manuals, the teacher collected tile and brick samples from companies on the district's architectural bid lists. To fulfill the community service requirements for the National Honor Society, students participated in a program where they learned about tesselation, then designed a bricked-in, tile-covered patio.

In both examples, the library media specialists reached beyond book learning to engage students in activities with real-life applications. They added variety to their own workday by conducting the programs outside their facility. Best of all, they initiated cross-curriculum cooperative teaching that diversified the program and lessened the burden on the media specialist.

Enrich Other Required and Elective Curricula

As a first-year English teacher introducing a concept that built on students' prior learning, I naively believed those who stared blankly at me and said, "We never learned that." When students whom I had taught the year before tried the same line, I knew better. Yet it wasn't until I became a library media specialist that I discovered just how repetitive explanations can be.

Consequently, although students theoretically know how to find books and use resources like the *Readers' Guide to Periodical Literature,* programs that focus on research techniques, reference books, or online databases are always worthwhile. New Internet or CD resources with unique navigation instructions make essential technology-based programs. Conversions to new computer systems require specific instructions so students can thereafter pursue independent research.

Adding new search tools? Changing from hard-bound resources like an encyclopedia or S.I.R.S. to their online versions? Anticipating a research project where students would benefit from being shown the best places to find information? All of these make perfect program topics. Although your patrons have frequented school library media centers for years, they still must learn what resources are available and how to use them. Programs on any such topics keep your media center running more smoothly while supporting curricula in every discipline.

Unique populations, like gifted and talented or special education students, often share the same curricula as their peers but require modifications. It is entirely appropriate, and sometimes necessary, to direct programs to their needs.

Fine arts electives offer myriad opportunities for programs. If you are near a big city, the local symphony, opera, or ballet company will send resource people and performers to schools for lectures and demonstrations. For off-campus programs, consider taking students to any of the aforementioned venues for a performance. Often for free or for a nominal cost, university drama departments have troupes that visit schools and perform everything from Shakespeare to mime. A program on music appreciation, either tightly structured like the rap music example developed for the language arts curriculum or more open-ended to appeal to band, choir, and choral students, can be fun and educational.

Student art displayed in the school library media center can be more than decoration. Enhanced by books about great painters, displays of biographies like Irving Stone's *Lust for Life*, or interactive bulletin boards where students match the painting with the artist, become programs that can remain intact as long as they draw in patrons. To add variety to this theme, set a date to end the display and replace it with a fresh one. Also, keep in mind that area university art departments may be good resources for obtaining works of art for display. For even more personal relevance to students, create displays of their work. Meet with your campus art teachers to schedule exhibits of different classes' art throughout the school year.

Provide Personal Enrichment

Nothing breaks the stereotypic misconception of the library as sterile, silent, and stuffy better than programs generated simply for students' personal enrichment. Because you interact with all grade levels and age groups, you know what interests students more than any other professional on campus. Topics that students request, books they check out consistently, and even the conversations that you interrupt to get students back on task provide clues for program topics. Also, you may distribute to potential target audiences surveys inquiring about their likes and dislikes. For program ideas, some media specialists display survey forms near a suggestion box in the school library media center.

As anyone who works with youth knows, some teen fads die quickly, whereas others maintain a perennial appeal. Although previous generations may have seen trends shift from month to month, today's teens have a much more minute-by-minute mentality. Peruse almost any teen magazine and you will find comparative lists with headings like "*Hot* Now, *In* Five Minutes Ago, *Out* Yesterday." The old adage "Here today, gone tomorrow" has never applied more literally. Generally, you can best serve yourself and your program audience by selecting a topic with lasting appeal. That way, you can update and repeat it in subsequent years. However, for target students who frequent the school library media center least (and probably need it the most), a timely, hot topic might generate interest and draw in students like no other.

Skateboarders who practice stunts over the wheelchair access ramps after school may not know about your nonfiction books like *Thrasher: The Radical Skateboard Book*. They may never have heard of Grady Grennan, the skateboarding protagonist of Randy Powell's ALA Best Book winner *Tribute to Another Dead Rock Star*. Although a standard geography or literature research paper is not likely to do more than frustrate these high-energy students, a program about extreme sports could certainly draw them in and perhaps, once they know what is available, motivate them to read.

Even though the focus of personal interest programs is usually fun, they can still be meaningful. Drama students are often glad to perform skits on drug awareness and sexual responsibility. Although the theme is serious, the context is entertaining, and the message is usually well received because it is shared by peers.

Ordering new books on a popular topic? A simple but attractive display can draw students in and get them reading. For one semester, I displayed several of Oprah's Book Club selections in book and audiotape formats beneath a colorful tri-fold board with Oprah's picture, reproductions of some of the book covers, and a tablet of reviews for different titles. Even though several books were much longer than the YA selections the students were used to, some students who seldom read at all checked out a book because they had heard about it on television. Although most of Oprah's selections are written for adults, similar book club ideas are being developed by school library media specialists throughout the country using YA books. (For great Web sites and more programming ideas, refer to the "Resources to Support Teen Interests" section of Chapter 6.)

Provide Professional Development for Teachers

As technology bulldozes ever deeper trenches into the world of education, teaching faculty new software programs and research tools has become a primary focus of inservice training. The need exists for every aspect of teaching, from accessing lesson plans on the Internet, to mastering new computerized grade books, to knowing how to incorporate multimedia presentations into classroom instruction.

Because school library media specialists are part of the decision-making committee on most campuses, they keep abreast of, or at least continually hear about, new technology, even that which may not apply to their specific job (like computerized attendance). As a result, they are in a position to either conduct inservice programs on the technology they know or co-host programs with experts qualified to offer training.

As many library media specialists will testify, general inservice sessions are almost always tailored to the needs of classroom teachers. Similarly, break-out sessions not created for or by media specialists seldom contain information that applies directly to running the school library media center. Rather than spending all that time in meetings that do not support your own professional needs, why not offer an inservice on computerized resources or an online program? Because teaching a subject requires you to learn it more thoroughly, offer a program on a new resource or interactive CD you have recently purchased. You'll be an expert by the time you use it with students.

Hosting inservices has several benefits. Besides providing a real service to teachers, it also empowers them to guide students through searches when they bring classes to the school library media center. Many districts offer professional growth hours for doing inservices. Even better, some districts pay inservice instructors a small stipend or give them compensation time equal to the number of hours it takes to prepare a presentation.

And the benefits continue. A natural result of providing meaningful inservices to faculty is good public relations for your media center. Media specialists who take an active role in helping teachers enhance their skills have an impact on their colleagues and make a good impression on the administration. Just as significantly, merely spending extended time with teachers develops rapport. Knowing your faculty helps you identify their needs, and letting them know you makes it easier to ask for their support when developing programs in the future.

Of course, programs created for faculty should not be limited to inservice days. Throughout the school year, you may offer a variety of mini-workshops (keep them to about 20 minutes, especially if they're offered after school when teachers are tired) on interesting topics. These sessions will probably not count toward inservice credit, but they will reap many of the same benefits of supporting your colleagues, enhancing your reputation, and promoting your media center.

To develop such programs, begin by asking faculty members what topics they would enjoy or what they need to enhance their effectiveness in the classroom. Some suggestions follow.

relaxation techniques that lower stress and improve health

dress for success (on a teacher's budget)

classroom arrangements for all learning styles

new computer programs

navigating online resources (for example, *S.I.R.S.*, *Newsbank*) introduction to grant writing

new reference resources available in the school library media center

the best YA author Web sites

customizing TV game shows for test reviews

self-esteem building exercises you can model for students

In addition to this list of topics, you can find related Web sites listed in Chapter 6 and detailed programs described in Chapter 8.

Benefits of Programming

Media specialists who incorporate special programs into their daily routine will reap many benefits. Programs offer opportunities to highlight the school library media center as well as the media center staff. Consequently, programming is an outstanding public relations vehicle for showcasing your media center and letting people see the talents, work, and creativity that go into presenting programs. Just as important, programming increases usage of the school library media center, supports and enriches classroom learning, broadens student and teacher interests, and inspires students to become lifelong learners.

Programs Enhance Public Relations

Special events generate great public relations. While consistently supporting staff and helping students establish a good rapport with patrons, programs also make strong impressions. Through programs, students are invited to change negative perceptions of their school library media center. Even students who enjoy reading may view the media center as a mere book repository or place where rigidity and silence are the order of the day. Vibrant programs enliven a facility. Attractive displays, interesting centers, and new, varied resources transform a drab setting into a stimulating learning environment.

Although revitalizing the physical surroundings may ignite a spark of interest in students, teachers will more quickly value the content of your contributions. Whether it is a multifaceted event in which several learning opportunities are transpiring simultaneously or a simple interactive bulletin board that introduces one teacher's upcoming unit, a program makes your facility the center of positive activity. A dreary environment is an invitation for restless students to stir up some excitement. With programs, you create the excitement and invite students to join you in unique learning experiences.

Programs Highlight the Media Specialist

One of the greatest annoyances for media specialists comes unwittingly from their own faculty. After simultaneously supervising three different classes, monitoring students on passes, circulating books, retrieving periodicals for students, and racing after the student whose latest thievery set off the security alarm, you pause between classes in the rare silence of the moment only to have a teacher enter with, "What a day! I should have been a librarian."

Unless they have done the job, others cannot know all the behind-the-scenes responsibilities required to run a library media center. But programs enable patrons to see first-hand the fruits of your efforts. They come to understand that, although the job demands are slightly different, your commitment to students and your creative contribution to their learning is the closest and probably the strongest professional support they have.

Through programs, students develop a better appreciation for the library media specialist as well. Instead of being only that voice repeating ad nauseam, "Log out of your program before leaving the computer," and "Please push in your chairs as you exit," you will become known as the host of that great event, or the person who recommended those new titles that got them reading or helped them survive a research assignment.

While maintaining their professionalism, some bolder media specialists strive to present themselves as genuine, accessible people. To introduce himself to patrons, one media specialist made a life-sized poster modeled after the author bios on bookflaps. Under a huge reproduction of his yearbook photo, he wrote his own brief biography, highlighting his education, hobbies, and favorite books. With a little ingenuity, he created a positive impression that increased students' willingness to use the media center and paved the way for more open and effective interactions throughout the year.

Programs Increase School Library Media Center Usage

Students gravitate toward fun, and they can have a good time at school without adults. To make their day enjoyable and meaningful, they need good teachers. To identify the best educators in a school, find the ones surrounded by students who look happy and act respectfully. Great teachers, and this term includes library media specialists, inspire students by sharing solid content in an engaging context. In the school library media center, that combination is best achieved through programming.

Good programs bring students into the media center and generally inspire them to return. Because all programs should include a selection of resources for further study, book circulation increases. Even those students who don't become regular patrons will at some point need to step back in to return a book they checked out. At that time, they may be drawn to an interest center or to a display that piques their curiosity.

Increased book circulation and patron usage also serve the media specialist financially. When you plan the following year's budget or request extra money for unique needs that inevitably arise, impressive circulation records and a well-frequented center are handy, persuasive tools for convincing your principal to grant financial requests.

Programs Support and Enrich Classroom Learning

Nearly every activity in the library media center enhances class work. Whether you present a program to broaden students' knowledge for an upcoming class unit, or, as is more often the case, to reinforce learning with follow-up activities, programs support and enrich classroom learning.

Direct or indirect support can be equally effective. Offering a brief presentation on a hard-to-find topic can provide invaluable support to classroom learning. For example, for classes reading *To Kill a Mockingbird,* presenting a brief program on where to find those almost nonexistent biographical resources on Harper Lee would be tremendously helpful. For that same unit, you could do a booktalk on Lee's contemporaries, including Carson McCullers, Flannery O'Connor, and Truman Capote, who was Lee's childhood friend and the inspiration for the character Dill in the novel.

Often, doing a program related to a new course in the curriculum can help generate interest in the class. Because instructors selected to teach the course may be tackling new curriculum themselves, collaborating with the instructors to present a program can help them clarify their course goals and help you decide what resources to order. Inevitably, the goal clarification and new resources enhance student learning.

In my own school, when a psychology elective was reintroduced after not being taught since the 1970s, working with the teacher helped us both. The resources I ordered gave her a richer background for teaching. Her lesson plans enabled me to order reference resources, books, and periodicals that targeted more specific learning objectives. In the end, our collaborative program on psychological disorders taught us both more about the subject, increased student involvement in the class, and revived circulation for books like Joanne Greenberg's *I Never Promised You a Rose Garden* and even short story collections from Poe to *Trapped! Cages of Mind and Body*.

Providing enrichment for classroom learning has many rewards. Media specialists who collaborate with teachers gain their support with increased patronage, better feedback when requesting input for purchasing new resources, and a generally more cooperative attitude when teachers bring students in for research. By making their job easier and more effective, you often inspire them to repay the courtesy.

Programs Broaden Student and Teacher Interest

Students with a passion for any subject will gladly research it incessantly. For confirmation, note how some students check the same sites on the library media center's computers daily. Perhaps it is a symptom of growing up in the cable television age, where they may see the same show or movie rerun countless times in any given week, but high school students today seem comfortable with the same kind of repetition enjoyed by preschoolers who are first learning new concepts.

There is so much for students to discover in the brief time they are in high school. All they have yet to learn becomes the perfect garden where new program ideas can grow. To find a program topic, brainstorm ideas beginning with a current student interest and keep "linking" to new possibilities until the ideal program topic materializes. Like site links on the Internet, students interested in Oscar de la Hoya could be introduced to information on famous Hispanic athletes, which could in turn teach them about athletes around the world, which could then lead them to information on the upcoming Olympic games.

The same principle can work for teachers. Often, new teachers participate in ice breaker activities at their first inservices to help them get acquainted with their new co-workers. After that, many teachers find a narrow niche and interact solely with their own grade level team, other teachers in their department, or those few teachers at their end of the hall with the same conference period. Programs directed at broadening teacher interest can do much for campus morale. Surveying teachers about their personal hobbies can inspire program ideas. Do some teachers belong to sewing or quilting circles? Display some of their work with arts and crafts books and a brief biography of the teacher. Better still, plan a program at which teachers can demonstrate their talents. Such programs affirm the contributing teacher and introduce students to interests that may be entirely new to them.

Have some faculty members won unique awards, or do they have unusual collections? Locked display cases would be ideal for sharing teachers' achievements or collections. Scanned copies of a stamp collection could tie in meaningfully with a history lesson on the subjects depicted on the stamps or the time period when they were first printed. Although not everyone wants to share original collections with even the most trustworthy library media specialist, others relish the opportunity to discuss their hobbies and teach students how to begin a collection of their own.

In addition to affirming colleagues and teaching new concepts to patrons, such programs cement your professional relationships with teachers. Personalizing connections between colleagues benefits both members professionally and sets an example for students about the importance of respecting co-workers and honoring their unique contributions.

Programs Inspire Lifelong Learning

Despite generations of dynamic and energetic exceptions, the favorite stereotype of our profession is still the drab, dowdy bore. It is remarkable how indelibly that image is etched into our culture. Even in the classic Christmas film, *It's a Wonderful Life,* George Bailey discovers that, had he never existed, his wife Mary would have ended up, of all horrible fates, a librarian. Racing to catch her as she closes the library, George does not find the radiant woman whose strength has held their family together in the worst of crises. Instead, wan, pathetic librarian Mary cowers from George until she shrieks in terror and faints helplessly in a crowd.

Even students who don't know the film, or the stereotype, seem to sense an undercurrent of sternness in library media specialists. During a guest appearance in a first-grade classroom where I was introduced as a high school librarian, I read the students a book.

After we finished the story, I told the children that books contain lessons that we can learn. "What message can we learn from reading this book?"

Hands shot up.

"Don't drop your book in the mud."

"Don't let your little sister play with library books. They're not toys."

"If you open the book too much, you'll break the spine."

Perhaps they didn't learn much from my question, but I did. I knew these students' library media specialist was a sweet, caring woman who was great with children. Yet, no matter how gentle our approach, students seem to interpret our being efficient and orderly as being strict and rigid.

Programs shatter that stereotype. Vibrant, fun, yet educationally sound events make school library media centers come alive. They revitalize a drab facility, invigorate the media specialist, and at their best, motivate students to read. For a generation whose brains are conditioned for multi-image, click-and-go stimuli, it's no wonder that some see a book as nothing more than a doorstop. We need not host multimedia extravaganzas just to get a book in students' hands, but we do need to reach them in ways that are meaningful. Handing a student a good book with your recommendation simply will not inspire a lifelong reader. But if you draw students to books through programs that pique their curiosity or challenge their intellect, you may well set them on a path of independent learning that can serve them for a lifetime.

Conclusion

There are many ways to find that initial spark of inspiration to begin library programming. Determine a topic or theme that you know will interest students. Consider the various formats that provide a creative outlet for teaching a new concept. Think of different audiences who could benefit from a program. Whatever lights that fire for you, let the ideas begin to flow. If your experience is anything like mine, one spark may help you discover the impact of programming and the value it offers for you and your patrons.

Chapter 2

Initial Stages of Program Planning

In general, program work can be divided into three stages: preparation, execution, and assessment. Each stage has concrete, manageable steps necessary for program success. Through experience, most people find unique approaches or modifications to the planning template. What works or seems most effective in one school or district may not be precisely how things are done in another. Nevertheless, the standards of detailed planning, protocol that emphasizes consideration of others, and some convenient shortcuts developed through experience all maximize the success of every program, even your first.

The two experiences to which I referred in Chapter 1 really did reframe how I perceived my role as a library media specialist. Students, in general, expressed a hesitation about, and sometimes an outright aversion to, reading. After the book giveaway for teachers, I recognized that my colleagues were drawn to the school library media center when I offered them something that they deemed useful. Although I couldn't imagine drawing students into my school library media center with giveaways, it became clear that I needed a dynamic hook to draw students into the school library media center and to pique their interest in reading. The solution was programming.

Truthfully, when I put together my first event, I did not even know it was formally called a program. Nor did I have a guide like this text to show me the steps for putting it together or assessing its effectiveness afterward. Instead, over the years I simply worked from instinct. Using my experience as a teacher and media specialist, I developed and refined events that ignited a spark of interest in my patrons. But the success of my first event convinced me that programming works. It even ignited a spark of creativity in me that secured my commitment to make programming an integral part of my job.

To introduce the step-by-step instructions for developing programs, Chapters 2 through 7 include brief segments of a scenario demonstrating the steps to program planning, shown in italics.

Gathering Ideas to Determine a Theme

Intrinsic Motivation

As my first goal, I set out to find a program idea that would excite students about learning. In high school, that's no small agenda. Initially, several possibilities came to mind. *The World's Best Thin Books* would meet the needs of my reluctant readers but was limited by the number of resources I had available. It also seemed merely to support the trend toward lowering my expectations that I was desperate to transcend. I'd read articles on censored books, hot topics, and award-winning novels that excited me, but they never seemed to have a unifying thread for nonreaders.

No, I needed something I was thrilled about presenting. From my years as a classroom teacher, I remembered that many students were willing to do their school work only because they were polite and respectful of their elders, not because they saw the value academics had in their lives.

That was it! As a teacher, I had shared self-esteem-building exercises in conjunction with many different units. I could do the same now, only on a larger scale. I began considering topics that I would enjoy sharing. Of the many ideas that came to mind, role models seemed the most appropriate and adaptable for different age groups, interest levels, and reading abilities. With a topic in mind, I could start researching its potential for being a successful program.

Gathering initial ideas and determining a specific program topic is the first of many steps to programming. With no set curriculum to follow, library media specialists are free to present any program topic that feels comfortable, personally inspires them, or drives them to excel.

Sometimes you may select a program because a particular timely issue has piqued students' interest, and current information is abundant. An examination of the electoral college is a recent example. Concerns about global warming and the shifts it has created in weather throughout the nation could serve as an effective topic almost anywhere. In Houston, consecutive winning seasons for the women's basketball team, the Comets, proved to be a fruitful program topic. As well as shattering old myths about female athletes' capacity to draw a diverse fan base, the WNBA's success invites great programs for fans, athletes, and sociology students.

At other times teachers' needs inspire program ideas. When a new teacher approached her school library media specialist about beginning a unit on forensics, they put together a program that offered concrete information in the context of a fascinating topic, serial killers. Students began their research on the FBI Web site (see Chapter 6), then explored the topic using science, social studies, and history resources.

Other media specialists have developed programs based on their personal interests. A conversation with Sandra Cisneros at a state conference prompted one media specialist in the Southwest to host a program on Hispanic writers that included the works of Gabriel García Márquez, Isabel Allende, Paul Martinez, and, of course, Cisneros.

No matter what topic you select, take the advice I give my students when they begin a writing assignment: If you're not interested in it, no one else will be either. Select a program topic because you are passionate about the subject, you see its value, or you are eager (or at least willing) to learn more about it yourself.

Informal Observation

Once you are enthusiastic about a topic, see if it has potential for any target audience. Start by making informal observations.

You can discover program topics in many places. While conversing with teachers, listen for their curriculum needs. Search your vertical files for ideas. Go through file cabinets where you store information on past units you've collaborated on with teachers. Examine course textbooks. Skim curriculum guides to refresh your memory of what skills and concepts they share. Finally, ask your assistant principal in charge of curriculum for practice tests or review sheets for end-of-course exams. Seeing what students must know can suggest many program possibilities.

As you prepare lessons with teachers who will bring their students in for research, watch for program ideas that spark enthusiasm. Casual conversations with colleagues may also lead to idea development. Interactions with staff over lunch will help you narrow your options. Most important, attendance at school meetings of all sorts will keep you in touch with school goals, student needs, and district plans. Because you probably already attend department chairperson meetings, consider joining some of the other faculty groups that meet. Individual department meetings reveal volumes about the strengths and needs within each discipline. Because it would be unrealistic to try to attend all meetings, be selective. With focus and attention, you can acquire many significant ideas from a single meeting.

If you're not comfortable just sitting in on such meetings, consider joining committees whose work affects the school. If your school has one, the site-based decision-making committee on your campus is probably every bit as influential as the administrative staff. If the responsibilities of that committee seem too heavy considering all your other duties, volunteer to be on the social committee. Members are almost always outgoing, and the emphasis of all their work is fun.

Faculty Suggestions

Rather than jumping into the planning stages of my role models program immediately, I sought feedback from my colleagues. At the next department chairperson meeting, I inquired what part of the population might benefit most from such a topic, and what approach would work best.

> Although their feedback was helpful, the core of my program did not solidify until I was mentoring a first-year English teacher who had no idea how to begin teaching *The Odyssey*. Instantly I was taken back to a lesson on personal heroes that I had created when I taught *Beowulf*. I had found a clearer program topic and a tentative title, "The Hero in You."

If you are included in the weekly department chairperson meetings, listen to teacher concerns and note new directions the district seems to be moving in philosophically. Ask teachers what units they find particularly challenging. Or, because most of the master teachers on your campus are probably also department chairpersons, ask them what original approaches they use to teach certain concepts. Throughout this stage, you need not explain why you are gathering ideas. Just casually inquire, then keep a file of notes for future reference.

Eventually, you may discover that a formal survey is in order. From that feedback you may see multiple ideas materializing into one program topic. My first attempt to garner teacher feedback drew a rather paltry number of responses. The problem was my approach. In subsequent years, instead of simply asking for feedback, which most teachers perceived as just one more task, I came up with the idea of making it a contest. In essence, I requested the same information as before, but this time, I gave them an incentive. (See Figure 2.1.)

Other Media Specialists' Expertise

> As I planned "The Hero in You," ideas flooded my way. Other library media specialists suggested available resources. One colleague told me she was personal friends with a famous baseball player who might be willing to serve as a guest speaker. Another had photographs from a tour through the upstairs warehouse in Amsterdam where Anne Frank and her family hid from the Nazis. When one colleague offered to display her Houston Comets T-shirt autographed by Cynthia Cooper, I recalled filling an entire folder with information on female athletes.

Although you may only meet once a month, or even just during district-wide faculty inservice days, other media specialists are perhaps your best resources outside your campus. Their shared experiences do more than give you common goals. They give you access to experts who, from experience, know what works in all facets of the job, including programming. Although some ideas shared in this text may work exactly as written for your students, others may need to be modified to fit the unique needs of your district. Your fellow media specialists can offer a wealth of information on what to watch for, including everything from strange glitches in your district's budgeting procedures for special events to knowing which local businesses underwrite program costs or provide volunteer presenters. Best of all, many will have first-hand experience with local guest speakers and visiting authors.

Participating in a computerized interlibrary loan program makes acquiring resources even easier. If your district doesn't subscribe to one, your media center colleagues can still provide extra materials for putting together a program or books to circulate after the program is complete.

WANTED: PROGRAM SUGGESTIONS

Would you like to determine how $500 of the school library media center book budget gets spent? Do you have a favorite author you want students to read? How about a hobby you'd like covered more thoroughly in our media center? Just give me your feedback and you're eligible to have those dream resources at your disposal. If your survey responses inspire my next program, I will order the resources you list at the end of the survey and reserve them for you first immediately after they arrive. Give five responses, determine $500 worth of new resources. What a bargain!

My students could use more information on

_____
_____
_____

I would be interested in seeing a program about

_____
_____
_____

A new topic or objective we are covering this year is

_____
_____
_____

If my students could learn only one thing, it would be

_____
_____
_____

If my suggestions inspire the next program, I would like you to order the following resources (you may highlight titles from catalogs or list topics, and I'll search for books for you):

_____
_____
_____
_____
_____
_____
_____
_____

Figure 2.1. Faculty suggestion survey.

Student Interests

Although I was growing more excited about my Heroes unit, I needed to ensure that my topic would really interest students. Prior success with the topic during my *Beowulf* unit gave me hope. But, for further reinforcement, I decided to experiment with circulation. I randomly pulled some books on heroes from my collection, including biographies on athletes ranging from Greg Louganis to Michael Jordan, books on heroes from the Holocaust that one teacher used for a unit on World War II, and even gods and mortals from mythology. Arranged under a colorful, mobile bulletin board I often use, I placed the display near the student suggestion box and student survey sheets to see how much attention the books would attract.

Pay close attention to the topics students research for personal interest and what issues students talk about among themselves. Keep in mind that subjects, such as sporting events or traditions of some school clubs, are new experiences for most students. If you can muster enthusiasm for what seem to be predictable student interests, you may create a program that can be repeated for many years.

Over the years, you may offer and refine programs covering topics with long-term student appeal. For example, an innovative media specialist in Seattle offers a program on legends, folklore, and fantasy that he modifies year after year. For a while, he says, unicorns were the trend. After *The Crucible* was released as a motion picture in 1997, the American literature teachers convinced him to shift the topic to the phenomenon of the witch trials, and the British literature teachers helped him incorporate elements of *Macbeth*, including a dramatic re-creation of the opening sequence. Just when the media specialist was ready to shift topics, *The Blair Witch Project* swept through the American psyche, and the topic took on a newer, more immediate relevancy.

Conversely, some student interests shift rapidly. The cutting edge is sharp, but it is also narrow. Therefore, if you pick a trendy topic, offer the program in a timely manner. If you hear that a specific interest is hot at Christmas time, you may be surprised to discover that students have cooled to it by spring break. On the other hand, if you have students that you're especially eager to reach, a program on their favorite hot topic might ignite a spark when nothing else will.

As with teachers, surveying students is an excellent way to discover what they like and what they want to know more about. Surveys like the example below can be given to homeroom or first-period teachers to distribute and collect at the beginning of the school year. If this seems too obtrusive, consider including this survey as part of any orientations you offer, or even work it into blocks of time when teachers bring in students for research. No matter how you share the survey initially, leave a stack of survey sheets beside a suggestion box in a prominent spot in your school library media center. Not surprisingly, your regular patrons will often be most enthusiastic and consistent about giving you honest feedback on the survey form.

STUDENT INTEREST SURVEY

Grade: _____   Sex: M _____   F _____

What are some of your favorite books?

_____

_____

_____

What hobbies, sports, and pastimes do you enjoy?

_____

_____

_____

What types of books do you enjoy reading?

Fiction	**Nonfiction**
_____ Realistic fiction	_____ General information
_____ Mystery	_____ Self-help/inspiration
_____ Science fiction	_____ Sports/recreation
_____ Fantasy	_____ Biography/true adventure
_____ Romance	_____ Social issues
_____ Horror	_____ History
_____ Poetry	_____ Religion/mythology
_____ Other (list below)	_____ Other (list below)
_____	_____
_____	_____
_____	_____

What subject areas interest you as program topics?
(Check all that interest you, or rank them from 1 to 10, 1 being your favorite.)

_____ Computers	_____ Science
_____ Inspiration/motivation	_____ Health and fitness
_____ Religions of the world	_____ The arts/entertainment
_____ Political and social issues	_____ Literature/authors
_____ Foreign languages/cultures	_____ History/biography
_____ Others (please list)	
_____	_____
_____	_____
_____	_____
_____	_____

Figure 2.2. Student interest survey.

Finally, if you pick a topic that is popular with young people and relatively new to you, let a few dependable students who love the topic help plan and execute the program. There are several benefits: They often are thrilled to work on the program, and their enthusiasm is contagious. Their word-of-mouth promotions will draw program participants you may not reach otherwise. And finally, they will help with accuracy. When preparing my program on rap music, I was abruptly corrected by a student aid for saying "rap singer" instead of the correct term, "rapper." Had I made that error during the program presentation, I would have lost credibility with my audience.

Curriculum Needs

Continuing to refine "The Hero in You," I spoke to the life skills instructor and discovered that learning to emulate a role model was not a separate, required skill taught in her curriculum. However, the idea was broad enough to tie in with several curricula. Athletics used examples of heroes in their training. The ROTC program cited examples of great soldiers and warriors and even hosted a guest speaker session with local Vietnam War veteran Roy Benavidez, who concluded his speeches by signing copies of his autobiography, *Medal of Honor: A Vietnam Warrior's Story*. A chemistry teacher allowed students who chose not to participate in the local science fair to write a report on a great scientist or inventor as an alternate assignment. I quickly discovered that my program idea tied into the curricula of many disciplines.

As stated previously, curriculum is a top priority in programming. Examining the school curriculum or focusing on specific subject area units lets you match program topics to required learning goals. Knowledge of scope and sequence—what topics are covered when—can prove valuable. Textbooks, curriculum guides, and vocational manuals include content information for every course. Opportunities for programs great and small abound. For example, media specialist Nancy Zajac realized a great opportunity when she found out that health classes were having a Red Cross representative come to the school to teach CPR. Working with health teachers, Nancy enhanced student learning by arranging for groups to visit one of two ambulances on display in the parking lot. There, emergency medical technicians explained what they did and demonstrated their new lifesaving equipment. Nancy extended learning by securing permission to arrange a display in the counselors' waiting area. It included brochures on local volunteer opportunities and a reminder to National Honor Society members and graduating seniors about community service requirements for membership and for some scholarship eligibility. She then tied together the program presentation, health class lesson, and community service theme with a display in her media center that included posters on lifesaving procedures and books, including the Community Service for Teens series.

Familiarity with the curriculum comes from serving on curriculum committees and attending grade-level meetings. Many administrators already include the media specialist. Others may have to be reminded how integral the library media specialist is to the school. Your extensive knowledge of existing policies and curriculum makes a credible argument for inclusion. Also, sharing information about the outstanding resources in the media center suggests that your library media center is essential to a successful school.

Be persuasive and become part of the school's decision-making team. The meetings will provide relevant information about curriculum needs and classroom activities. They are also the perfect forum for generating program ideas. In the end, everyone benefits from the collaborative effort. The curriculum is enriched and supported, brainstorming sessions are more fruitful, resource circulation increases, and student learning is enhanced.

Professional Development Activities

Attending conferences, workshops, and courses in your school district and at universities can enhance program development. By looking for ideas or special topics at such events, you will quickly discover that program ideas appear everywhere. A media specialist in California reported that her program for English and reading teachers, "Hot Topics in YA Fiction," resulted from her attendance at a reading conference.

Professional journals and teacher magazines are excellent sources for event ideas. Reading about programs that worked for someone else may motivate you to design a similar program or develop a more elaborate one on the same topic.

Perusing professional collections at the district or campus level can suggest program themes and reveal more resources. During the planning stage of "The Hero in You," I visited my district teacher center and found books and the entire series of Stephen Covey videos that our superintendent had ordered when she attended Covey's "7 Habits" training.

Community Happenings

Local events can trigger program ideas. Special holidays, festivals, fairs, and cultural activities can suggest topics for school library media center programs. Community organizations, universities, bookstores, and museums often host special programs that can generate program ideas and provide resources. Knowing the dates and speakers involved in such activities is essential for tying programs to community events. Outstanding programs can result from all types of local events, such as the Strawberry Festival in Pasadena, Texas, or a hot air balloon extravaganza in Albuquerque, New Mexico. The latter event inspired one perceptive media specialist to imagine how well the local "Balloon Fest" could translate into a fun-filled school library media center program. Beyond just observing and teaching about hot air balloons exclusively, she broadened her topic to include both a history lesson on the technological evolution of aviation and transportation and a science lesson on gravity and gases. Clearly, ideas, approaches, and formats for any subject are endless.

Besides events, special holidays make excellent program topics. Bored with the usual Thanksgiving, Christmas, and Valentine themes? Use programs to help students learn about elections or veterans in November, Martin Luther King Jr. in January, and Mexico's traditions and history on Cinco de Mayo.

Looking for topics with more immediacy for students? Check out upcoming local events. When are they going to happen? Who is involved? Answers to these questions are rife with program possibilities. Keep up with the local newspaper, magazines, radio, and television, where program ideas abound. Seeking a more direct approach? Call the local chamber of commerce and request the community calendar of events. Contact the community events coordinator. You may carry over some events to your library media center. Such contacts also result in positive publicity for your school. Discovering that a nationally recognized antique road show had just passed through her city, media specialist Sherry Lynn Bodnar decided to develop an antiques display. After several theme shifts, her final antique show became a program for the math department that taught the evolution of counting machines. Display items donated by teachers and local citizens included an ancient abacus, a turn-of-the-century cash register, slide rules, a manual adding machine, solar-powered calculators, and even a sliding grade point averaging chart made of cardboard that one teacher sheepishly admitted to still using.

Vast community resources, including special events, people, places, and things, give you valuable support when determining themes and planning your program. Chapters 4 and 5 list various types of community resources for generating program ideas, and Chapter 6 provides Internet sites for the community resources.

Developing a Specific Plan

Good planning requires clarity. Be systematic. Narrow the scope of what you will cover. Decide precise program goals. Specify exactly who will attend. Then gather resources. Abundant materials at your immediate disposal will invite endless possibilities. As you gather ideas, those resource options will be invaluable. By phase two of program planning, where you develop and narrow your theme, you can weed out excess.

To mold general ideas into a concrete, workable plan, answer the following questions:

- What are my general goals for the program?
- Whom (grade, age, gender) will this topic interest?
- What format (displays, centers, speakers) will I use for this program?
- Where will I find available resources on the topic?
- What are the best date and time to offer the program?
- What will the logistics be for carrying out this program?

Setting Goals

After specifying a theme and outlining program ideas, develop clear goals. Begin with the end in mind. List the precise purposes for the program. What final results will participants derive from the program? When developing the goals, relate every one either to curriculum or to the personal interests of students and faculty. Programs based on such goals are unquestionably relevant to participants. Writing the goals in lesson plan format structures the planning process and clarifies the core of your program.

The best programs use a combination of approaches. For "The Hero in You," I drew from many sources.

By brainstorming and discussing with faculty, I refined my ideas so that my topic would be most relevant and my presentation more effective. Knowledge of curriculum, student interests, professional resources, and community events proved essential in generating specific ideas for program development. Now I was ready to move on to the next stage, clarifying the goals for my program, "The Hero in You."

After much consideration, I specified my program goals:

- I will share traditional heroic stories from different historical periods.

- I will offer students an opportunity to determine what qualities they deem heroic.

- I will help students identify role models for the qualities, skills, or professions they admire.

- I will introduce students to community mentors and local heroes.

- I will familiarize students with self-esteem-building resources.

Considering the Audience

Although hosting a general assembly sounded like fun, it also seemed like a logistical nightmare. Remembering the amount of explanation and follow-through required in my *Beowulf* heroes unit, I knew I could not offer an effective program by opening the school library media center to just any students. I had to narrow my focus.

Several options came to mind. I could pick a target audience. I could limit examples to one scholastic discipline. I could select a single subject, or even a specific class. As ideas ricocheted through my head, I realized that starting with a small target group would enable me to develop and refine my program while still allowing me to expand it to reach more students if I chose to do it again in the future. After studying the content of my program ideas thus far, I selected two divergent groups of students that I thought would benefit most from the topic: European history students and special reading classes.

When developing programs for students, match the theme to the age, interests, and gender of the audience. Although occasionally planning a program for all students in the school can be appropriate, targeting a specific segment of the population, such as the gifted and talented students, vocational classes, or seniors enrolled in advanced placement courses, ensures several benefits for the students and you.

Limiting your audience to a specific group lets you fulfill their learning needs more directly. Also, events for smaller populations are easier to schedule. It would be unrealistic to plan huge extravaganzas every month. However, you could potentially offer programs monthly by planning small group events or choosing simple program ideas from Chapter 8.

Matching the appropriate audience to the topic is essential. After specifying your topic and planning your program activities, ask yourself the following questions:

- Is my topic appropriate for my audience?
- Will the topic pique the audience's interest?
- Are the length and content of the activities appropriate for the audience's maturity level?
- Will the planned activities hold their attention?
- What prior knowledge must my audience have to participate fully in the program?
- What new knowledge will they gain from it?

Your target audience can also be faculty or parents. Programs for faculty (some are shared in Chapter 8) may cover professional growth topics ranging from technology to reference materials to young adult literature. During a faculty workshop titled "What They're Reading," a media specialist in Wisconsin presented booktalks on the most frequently circulated books in her collection. Her 20-minute program familiarized teachers with her collection and informed them about students' personal interests.

As a book reviewer for the American Library Association's *Booklist*, I have also hosted programs on book reviewing. Whether as an inservice presentation to help colleagues with collection development or as a tool to help parents or teachers select resources appropriate for teens, this program is consistently popular and effective.

Parents are frequently asked to volunteer to work at programs or events, but they are seldom invited as guests. They are great, appreciative audiences. With the counseling team, offer a program informing parents about new classes being offered, new co-curricular programs sponsored by local junior colleges, or scholarship opportunities for their children. For technology, teach parents how to use computer resources that allow for remote access at home.

Besides topics that primarily benefit students, some programs can address parents' needs. During homecoming week, host a nostalgic program. After Christmas break, offer one on goal setting or healthy weight loss regimens. In spring, invite an accountant to share tax tips. As you reach out to the community and generate good PR for your school, programs for parents also give you a welcome diversion from your routine.

Determining a Time Frame

Early in the planning process, determine a time frame for your event. Often, other factors dictate the length of your program. Some time frames are predetermined because of your audience. If you offer a program to faculty during the school day, it must be short so they can attend during their conference period.

Program format can also determine time frames. Video presentations, for example, last as long as the segment you choose to show. Demonstrations last as long as it takes the presenter to share a process. Guest speakers may determine how long they can stay or how much information or expertise they have to share. Displays and exhibits may not require a set time but may simply be available for students to view or interact with whenever they choose. Most often, program time frames are set by the school bell schedule. Except for special programs that you schedule like field trips and pull students from their regular classes, confine programs to single class periods, factoring in the time it takes for students to arrive and settle down.

Identifying Resources

Looking for biographical resources on heroes in my collection, I realized what a cross-curricular topic I had chosen. I found inspiring stories of athletes, religious figures, artists, philosophers, scientists, and political and military leaders. Searching further, I determined several avenues for program presentations that I could take.

In the 100s alone I had inspirational books like Dr. Seuss's *Oh, The Places You'll Go!*, a book checked out each year as students prepared graduation speeches. We had *Do It! Let's Get Off Our Buts* and *Life 101* by John-Roger and Peter McWilliams. Because our superintendent loved the Stephen R. Covey training, we had Covey's *7 Habits of Highly Effective People* and his son Sean's complementary text, *7 Habits of Highly Effective Teens.* We had several editions of *Chicken Soup for the Teenage Soul,* which I knew students loved because, next to the *Guinness Book of World Records,* they are the most circulated books in my collection.

In the reference section I found *Heroes of Conscience, The 100 Most Influential Women of All Time,* and *Heroes of the Holocaust.* Clearly, I already had the book resources I needed to share with my students during the program. Yet so many other types of resources—people, display items, media—are also key elements to program success. From my book collection alone, I had numerous resources available on my topic. After developing my program itinerary more clearly, I could determine other resources.

With clear program goals, a target audience, and a specific time frame, you can identify appropriate materials. To select resources, consider the following:

    age of audience

    maturity level of audience

    interest level of audience

    audience's background knowledge of topic

    content of material

    appropriateness of material for a school program

    appropriateness of material for program format

    currency of resources

    accessibility of resources

    availability of supporting resources on topic

When identifying program resources, also consider the region where you work. Resources for a program about the rodeo are plentiful in Houston, which sponsors one of the largest livestock shows and rodeos in the world. Similarly, motion picture resources would be more accessible to schools in southern California, and equipment for aquatic themes could be found in either tropical areas or along any coast where fishing and sailing are major industries. Keep in mind that each geographic region contains abundant resources that can make static presentations come alive with hands-on access to materials.

Various types of resources can support programming. Media software, young adult literature, professional books, exhibits, and displays are among the most frequently used resources. In addition, teacher-made and student-generated resources are readily available to enrich media center programs. Because this topic includes so much information, Chapter 4 is devoted to identifying and locating resources.

Choosing a Format

As mentioned previously, time and format interrelate. Format often dictates preparation time and program length. Programs range from simple displays to sophisticated full-day or ongoing events. Each format listed in this section offers tremendous flexibility. Programs of any type can be as simple or as elaborate as you desire. To select your format, consider time, audience, facility space, and established goals. Simple programs usually require only a single format. Elaborate events often incorporate several formats to vary activities and meet multiple program goals.

Exhibits and Displays

Exhibits and displays are the most frequently used form of programming in school library media centers. Surprisingly, however, many media specialists do not realize that this common format constitutes a program. When discussing our book with media specialists, one claimed that she had not developed a program in years. However, in a subsequent conversation, she described an activity she developed with student art. As mere decoration, artwork is not a program. But by adding a learning component, she made it one. Simply displaying books on art technique and offering supplemental materials (brochures about nearby art museums, information about local artists' exhibits) near the students' work transforms an aesthetically appealing exhibit into an effective and easy-to-prepare program.

Exhibits and displays can be designed for most themes, whether supporting curriculum or personal interests. Common forms include:

> bulletin boards
>
> wall displays
>
> mobiles
>
> display cases
>
> display shelves
>
> table exhibits
>
> freestanding displays
>
> traveling trunks

Exhibits and displays serve many functions. Some media specialists use them to feature different topics in the school library media center each month. Others create them to supplement large presentations. Before a major program, exhibits and displays introduce key concepts or pique students' curiosity. During the event, they enhance the presentation. When used as follow-up activities after a program, they reinforce or extend learning. Finally, they are the perfect place to display books related to the program topic.

Photo 2.1. At Clear Lake High School in Texas, Anne Clancy, Fran Studdard, and Linda Wright support Banned Books Week with a program enhanced by displays and decorations throughout the library media center.

Because of their simplicity and familiarity, these formats make perfect first programs. Display cases, table displays, or bulletin boards attract patrons to the school library media center. Although they are usually the least time-consuming to construct, they require good planning. Remember, placing items in a display case or hanging art on a bulletin board is not programming; you need a learning component.

Plan your displays around a particular topic; develop learning objectives; then create an activity, quiz, game, or assignment that allows students to demonstrate mastery. Most displays are aesthetically appealing, but they must also be rich in content. Label objects with titles and include descriptions to enrich student vocabulary. Provide curriculum-related information. Include challenging activities that inspire patrons to explore further reading opportunities.

Exhibits and displays are particularly useful for attracting students who would not otherwise want to visit the school library media center. Intriguing displays may draw reluctant students into the media center and invite them to explore what it can offer. Ideally, these students may even check out a book on the topic.

For information about identifying special exhibits and displays to meet specific thematic needs, refer to Chapter 4. For step-by-step instructions about constructing displays, read *3-D Displays for Libraries, Schools and Media Centers* by Earlene Green Evans and Muriel Miller Branch (2000).

Featured Speakers and Entertainers

Well-chosen guest speakers can make programs dynamic. You may invite one or several speakers to share information on a single topic. At a recent school library media center event, for example, an airline pilot visited the media center to teach vocational students about her profession. In a similar but more involved program, a military pilot, a private pilot, and a commercial airline pilot were the featured speakers for the ROTC cadets.

Programs featuring guest speakers offer several format options:

- single speaker presenting the topic to one group
- single speaker presenting the topic multiple times to various groups
- multiple speakers presenting their topics to one group
- multiple speakers presenting their topics multiple times
- multiple speakers presenting their topics in different areas of the facility at the same time

Interest Centers

Some teachers, especially in the sciences, routinely construct classroom interest centers to supplement, reinforce, and enrich a unit. Consider using this form of programming in the school library media center. Like exhibits and displays, interest centers attract students. They supplement and extend class curriculum; they can also provide activities following special programming events. Although they serve the same purpose as exhibits, interest centers are usually more elaborate. They often include several activities, supporting posters, instructions, artwork, and other resources. You can build them in individual carrels, on table tops, within divider units, or in any space large enough for independent or small group activities. You may erect them throughout the library media center. Interest centers should include intriguing items that stimulate thought and prompt discussion among students. For example, an aquarium in the media center set up and maintained by the science club can be the focal object for an interest center that provides activities on sea life or environmental issues.

Steps for setting up a learning center follow:

1. Select a versatile theme or topic. (You may want to leave the center up for a long time.)

2. Precisely define the goals.

3. Select your resources.

4. Use durable materials.

5. Make the setup functional and aesthetically appealing.

Find unique places to set up your interest center. For example, media specialist Debra Chicowlas transformed an unused study carrel into a twentieth-century history center. Dedicating each of six spaces to a different decade, she developed history trivia games and interactive activities. Her students especially loved the interactive elements, including a 1950s tabletop juke box that, at the push of a button, supplied answers to questions posed about McCarthyism, the Eisenhower administration, and the history of rock and roll. Wisely, Debra included book displays in each carrel. As a result, classics from each decade that hadn't been checked out for years began circulating again.

When identifying stimulating learning center activities, consider topics that will interest students, such as

aviation center	detective center
computer center	career center
music center	sports center
fantasy center	farming center
art center	ecology center
interior design center	folklore center
crafts center	author center

Demonstrations

During most of these programs, you, or a guest speaker, will demonstrate a process in person. However, you may also invite students to the school library media center to view a previously filmed demonstration. Your program can include one or multiple demonstrations. For one program in Ohio, a local artist discussed and demonstrated the art of silk-screening. Afterward, the media specialist hung samples of the artist's work throughout the media center, and art teachers followed up with classroom lessons in which students created their own silk-screen designs. The program was so successful that the media specialist expanded it the following year by inviting three different artists to demonstrate their unique art techniques: silk-screening, painting with watercolors, and graphic designing on a computer. For this particular program the media specialist established three different centers (or stations). Small groups of students visited each center, learned about the art technique, viewed the display of art forms, and took part in hands-on activities planned by each artist.

Demonstrations can be developed around most any theme, such as

cooking	using computer software
silk screening	cartoon drawing
dancing	puzzle solving
baking	scrapbook (or "memory book") designing
Internet communicating	learning CPR
exercising	building birdhouses

Media Programs

As a movie buff, I thought of several feature films that would appeal to students and tie in with my heroes theme. After considering many possibilities, I decided to show *White Squall*, an outstanding film about a group of teen boys whose semester at sea turns tragic, forcing them to demonstrate heroism to survive and strength of character to face the aftermath. Because I could not incorporate a two-hour film into my program, I offered two showings of the film after school on the days prior to my program.

Commercially produced media materials abound and can support almost any thematic program. Films, recordings, and computer software that focus on YA books and authors, community resources, special holidays, and other topics can become programs or program components. Media presentations also make effective professional development programs for faculty.

Conclusion

Formats should accommodate program needs, interests, and goals. Your time frame dictates how you will achieve those goals. Begin the process of putting together your program with learning objectives in mind. New facets to your program and unexpected resources will inevitably improve your original plan. Modify as necessary. As the expert, you will know what changes will enhance your program and make it greater than you originally thought possible.

Chapter 3

Final Stages of Program Planning

With my focus and target audience determined, I started creating a plan for developing my program, "The Hero in You." To reach students from two very divergent groups, European history and special reading classes, I kept my focus rather general. At first I was concerned. Was I casting my teaching net too broadly and thus losing effectiveness? But the disparate audiences resulted in a generic approach that, I discovered in later years, could be modified to reach many different student populations.

Browsing through the resources that I'd gathered on the topic, I noticed several attractive, recently published books on the legends of King Arthur. While reading, I looked up and noticed that I have all round tables in my library media center. The idea of hosting a medieval event sounded fun, but ultimately unmanageable. However, because I was targeting mostly history students as my audience, I thought, "Why not do the program as a timeline?" I could divide the library into sections, covering heroes from different periods in history, culminating in the personalized hero of today.

After much legwork and further modification of ideas, my program took shape. In each section, I would highlight one hero who excelled in a forum different from all the others:

1. Section one: Crusaders. Joan of Arc was my main focus, because she linked early history, religion, and women.

2. Section two: Visionaries. From literature, Don Quixote served as a Spanish role model. (My school population was 75 percent Hispanic, with nearly every student in the special reading class an ESL student with little English proficiency.)

3. Section three: Risk-takers. Nineteenth-century freedom fighter Harriet Tubman was my prime example.

4. Section four: Champions. Cynthia Cooper, Sammy Sosa, and Tara Lipinski were three of several contemporary sports figures highlighted.

5. Section five: "You." Through this program, students would learn how the heroic qualities introduced related to them.

Outlining the Program Content

After deciding your theme, goals, audience, time frame, and available resources, determine the specific content for your program. Making this decision at this point enables you to select only the most relevant resources.

With your content and goals in mind, begin your research. Talk to teachers, examine reference materials and professional resources, and explore the burgeoning data available on the Internet. During this stage, ideas will begin to solidify into a concrete program plan. A clear vision invites better communication and allows you to ask the right questions for securing resource persons, businesses, organizations, and potential helpers.

Obtaining Administrative Approval

You are probably free to create curriculum-related programs formatted as centers, exhibits, or displays without requesting permission. But larger events that incorporate guest speakers or rented exhibits require administrative approval. Know district policies for sponsoring major events. What chain of command must you follow? The first step usually is obtaining the principal's permission.

After choosing the theme and having a general vision of program content, share your ideas and goals with the principal. School districts are often concerned about specific themes and content of programs, particularly those not directly related to the school curriculum. Keep the principal apprised of all upcoming events. Always let him or her know about program plans, focusing especially on the positive PR they generate for the school.

Following every visit, send a memo outlining your discussion and thanking the principal for his or her time and receptivity. Just as important, invite the principal to every program. For smaller events, informally ask the principal to visit your library media center. When hosting an elaborate program, send your principal a written invitation. Even if the principal slips in for a brief moment to observe a sliver of a presentation or view a display of students' work, including the principal establishes a positive rapport. Over time, even a handful of small programs can make a lasting impression.

Principals are usually pleased when their media specialist takes the initiative to develop special programs for students and teachers. Although secondary level principals may not have the time to collaborate with the media specialist on programs as some elementary principals do, they may show their support through promotion and even financial backing. Naturally, funding from the principal can enable you to achieve many program goals that would otherwise strain your budget or be unattainable.

I kept my principal apprised at every major stage of my program planning. When requesting initial feedback from colleagues at department chairperson meetings, I continually included the principal (and assistant principal in charge of curriculum) in the discussion. After I determined the general plan described above, I brought a copy marked "draft" to my principal. Rather than presenting it as a plan set in stone, I simply asked him to look over the draft and offer any ideas for improving the concept.

Consulting him before moving forward with my plans was essential to the program's success. Knowing about the program throughout the planning stages allowed him to mention the event to teachers on our campus and administrators throughout the district. Although he came up with no suggestions on the content or format, he kept finding new ways in which I might promote the event. He brought samples of different district circulars, introduced me to our district's public relations coordinator, and asked me to share my program planning strategies with library media center colleagues at the following year's inservice.

Securing Teacher Support

Successful programs need faculty support. Throughout the development stages of program planning, request teacher input for the upcoming event. Their feedback can improve your program markedly. Contributing teachers develop a sense of ownership and excitement about the event, which can help generate school-wide anticipation. Simple marketing strategies such as the following can generate great enthusiasm for the project:

- Share the upcoming program idea with the faculty involved.
- Encourage faculty to suggest program ideas and create related classroom activities.
- Provide faculty with sample activities related to the program.
- At a faculty meeting, share with teachers the program theme and plans for the specific target group.
- Inform faculty that you will continue making program announcements throughout the planning process.
- Finally, to avoid resistance from uninvolved parties, invite all colleagues to suggest program ideas that you might explore in a future program.

Planning the Specific Details

This next planning phase is often the most difficult. Determining a time, date, and location for your event depends on many factors, including the rigid schedule to which most schools must adhere. Factoring in the challenge of scheduling human and material resources, potential conflicts increase. Fortunately, you are accustomed to handling multiple responsibilities simultaneously and working around others' less flexible time constraints. As a result, this stage requires only some extra planning and creative negotiating.

Select and Verify a Location

After obtaining the principal's approval and support, choose the best location for your program. Your school library media center will accommodate most events. While fulfilling learning objectives, your program also publicizes the media center. By inviting students into the facility for a riveting program, you encourage them to view your media center as a vibrant hub of activity filled with interesting materials. Sometimes such events encourage students who rarely frequent the school library media center to return later to browse through materials or view displays; checking out a book is not always required.

Some programs demand a unique setting outside the school library media center. For example, a traveling Shakespearean troupe might need the auditorium. Consider on-campus options such as classrooms, labs, the school patio, or even the ballfield. You may also schedule events off campus, as did a North Carolina media specialist who organized a program for faculty at the district professional library. Handle off-campus programs as you would a field trip: Secure transportation, complete appropriate permission slips, and adhere to other district rules and policies.

Choose and Confirm a Date and Time

Having worked on the same campus for over ten years, I already knew general patterns for scheduling the media center. Speech classes came in the second week of every grading period. Sophomores wrote author research papers before spring break, juniors did career research in the fall, and seniors composed abstracts during the last one-third of each semester. Consequently, I scheduled my event between those established routines. Then I confirmed that no one else had planned conflicting events for that day. If history or reading students were released from class for a field trip or assembly on my program day, I could completely miscalculate the size of my program audience.

Scheduling an event is like constructing a three-dimensional puzzle. All facets must align and interlock or the entire structure collapses. So, at the earliest reasonable opportunity, secure a precise date for your program. Reaching that concrete decision, however, requires first selecting several tentative dates and times that might work, then coordinating them with other campus events on the school calendar. Determine two possible dates that do not conflict with other school programs, then investigate the following factors:

> school schedule (classes, lunch, passing periods)
>
> availability of resource persons
>
> availability of faculty
>
> availability of support personnel, including volunteers and aides
>
> availability of resource materials that support the presentation

With these restrictions in mind, schedule small programs at least four to six weeks ahead of the program date. Schedule the extravaganzas several months in advance.

Working around the school calendar, and particularly class schedules, is another major obstacle to planning. As an educator, your experience working around class, lunch, athletics, and fine arts schedules will help you choose the best date. To secure backing from teachers, discuss the matter thoroughly with colleagues at department chairperson, subject area, and faculty meetings. Clearly, two major purposes for having a program are to create positive impressions of the library media center and to improve its effectiveness in the school. Understandably, most teachers do not appreciate disruptions to their schedule. By asking for their input as you schedule the event, you engender a positive attitude toward you, the program, and your library media center. Without question, teachers' support helps secure some of the pieces of that scheduling puzzle.

Select and Schedule Guest Speakers

Who are the best speakers for special events? Your local community is filled with possibilities. Chapter 4 includes useful information about locating them. Chapter 6 goes a step further and lists numerous Web sites of authors, publishers, and other resources that can connect you with speakers.

Selecting appropriate speakers is critical for programming. Above all, guest speakers must be interesting to students. Their content should be engaging and appropriate to the age level of the audience. With your professional experience, you can determine quite a bit about the potential speaker's ability to relate to teens. Professionals who exude energy and authority make vibrant, often entertaining presenters. Programs that incorporate guest speakers depend entirely on the effectiveness of the person you select. Therefore, know the intended speaker.

Most of us have listened to excruciatingly dull speeches or abysmal presentations by speakers with poor communication skills. The topic may have been relevant, the material well organized and useful, but the speaker simply could not connect with the audience. For adults, that can be frustrating. With teens, it can be disastrous. Even speakers with solid professional credentials, an impressive body of knowledge, and plenty of speaking experience may not be the best choice for high school students. Consequently, prior to the program, determine whether the resource person is a good match for your patrons.

How can you make that decision with confidence? No strategy is foolproof, but certain practices in the business world apply here. Although requesting a resume or letters of recommendation is unnecessary in this context, the principles behind them work. Choose people with experience speaking to teens. Guests who talk down to them, even unintentionally, can undermine all of your program preparation. To avoid this problem, get recommendations from colleagues who have already heard the speaker, or inquire about the speaker's prior engagements. Follow up on that request by calling the previous host. Courteously inquire about the general success of the program and about the guest speaker's strengths. By keeping the conversation positive, you make the previous host comfortable with sharing honest feedback. Whenever possible, meet with the potential speaker prior to making a definite commitment. During your conversation, keep the following questions in mind:

- Is the speaker knowledgeable about the topic?
- Will the speaker be interesting to teens?
- Has the speaker worked with teens before?

- Does the speaker seem to grasp the focus and purpose of my program?
- Have others recommended this speaker?
- Is the speaker genuinely willing to work within the program demands?

As a general rule, the most important question to consider is: If I were a student required to sit through this speaker's presentation, would I enjoy it as well as learn from it?

When selecting a guest speaker for "The Hero in You," I thought about how difficult it can be to impress a teen. If Cynthia Cooper or Tiger Woods stepped into my school library media center, students would automatically be impressed. But I had no resources for acquiring a superstar for my program, so I needed to select guests who commanded student attention through their speaking talents, their credentials, and their expertise.

To find speakers, start searching near the school. The local community is filled with resource possibilities. County and city officials can make strong impressions on students. Artists, musicians, and athletes hold special intrigue for many teens. Professionals at nearby businesses are often glad to share their time and expertise. Parents are also a wellspring of information. Refer to Chapter 4 for more suggestions about finding guest speakers.

The speaker's availability is a major consideration for program planning. When first meeting or conversing with potential speakers, find out when they will be available to participate in the program. If you have already chosen a date and location, share that information. If the date conflicts with the speaker's schedule, suggest the alternate date still open on the school events calendar.

After selecting a speaker, share the following program details:

> date and time
>
> location of presentation
>
> program goals
>
> program content
>
> length of the program
>
> age of the audience
>
> size of the audience
>
> equipment and software needs (including microphone)
>
> accessory needs (such as podium, screen, dry board and markers)

One week prior to the event, help your guest speaker by

- Providing a final written reminder of date, time, and location;
- Reiterating the importance of being on time;
- Reminding him or her of the amount of time allotted; and
- Confirming equipment and requested resources.

Finally, follow up with a telephone call several days before the event to ensure that the speaker knows and can honor his or her commitment. Clarify again equipment needs and answer any final questions the speaker may have.

Because guest speakers are integral to your program, obtaining a firm commitment from them solidifies the tentative plans made earlier. Immediately after guest speakers confirm their participation, lock in the program time on the school calendar. Because so many special events occur throughout a school year, other faculty members may be vying for some of those same times. Confirming a date frees up your alternative choice for colleagues waiting to plan a special event (like a sports tournament, fair, or field trip).

Choose and Provide for Support Personnel

After selecting the main guest speaker, find and secure any other participants needed to carry out the program. You may need other guest participants, parent volunteers, and faculty members to help shoulder the responsibilities of executing your program. The number of students attending and number of activities planned are the two main criteria for determining how many presenters and helpers you need.

Finding volunteer help is similar to, yet not quite as demanding as, selecting primary guest speakers. Some larger schools may have enough staff members employed in the school library media center to shoulder all the supporting tasks, like ushering students in and out of the facility, operating equipment, and helping presenters with their displays and demonstrations. Regardless of their role, volunteers are essential members of your program team. Well before the program day, meet with all staff members and volunteers to give them information about the topic being presented. Assign each volunteer a specific task for which he or she is in charge. Then take the time to review with volunteers their responsibilities. Let them ask questions. Although staff members may know how you run the school library media center, where everything is, and how it works, volunteers may be new to your campus or to participating in programs. Help them feel secure. When they do, they can be more productive and effective.

Finally, ensure that each individual can relate to students. Although not as critical as the main guest speaker who will be commanding the students' attention, other participants help set the tone for the event. Volunteers who help students feel comfortable and successful will greatly enhance the impression students come away with by program's end.

Select, Order, and Schedule Resource Materials

Materials to support the program include books, reference materials, professional materials for teachers, media, computer and audiovisual equipment, Internet Web sites, exhibits, displays, and any other materials related to the topic. (Chapter 4 focuses on identifying resources.) Begin searching for support materials on the topic within your own school library media center, other media centers within the district, and the district professional library (if one is available). Then search the community for resource persons, businesses, and organizations that can provide support materials. When necessary, purchase books and materials related to the topic.

Being familiar with existing resources on your topic allows you to select, order, and/or schedule the materials. It is entirely appropriate to plan some programs around topics for which you already have great resources. This approach is especially helpful if your budget is extremely limited. When selecting resources, ask yourself:

- Is the content of the resource related to the program theme?
- Is the resource appropriate for the age level of the target group?
- Will the resource interest the target group?
- Is the resource current?
- Is the resource easily accessible?
- What is the cost of the resource (if any)?

Some media specialists begin planning an event a year in advance, particularly when they are planning an extravaganza such as a special anniversary of their school. This advanced planning enables you to budget for books and media in advance or reserve freestanding exhibits and multimedia programs.

While searching for displays, I recalled visiting a theater shop in Toronto that carried playbills, posters, and decorations advertising different shows, including *Man of La Mancha*. Although ordering something directly from that store wasn't financially feasible, I initiated a new search over the Web, where I was able to purchase an eye-catching, three-dimensional cardboard display from the movie to display in my Visionaries section. Thanks to a little forethought, I was able to share expenses with my school's drama teacher, who split the cost of the display on the condition that she get to keep it in her classroom after the program was completed.

Soon I was adding new program elements to the event. For the Risk-takers segment, I found a parent volunteer willing to share his experience as a mountain climber. Not only did he have mountain climbing gear to bring for his presentation, but he also enlarged to poster size two attention-grabbing photos of him dangling from a mountainside.

Develop Contingency Plans

Be prepared to troubleshoot when unexpected challenges arise. Prepare alternate plans and backup activities. For smaller programs, also determine another date to present your program in case an unforeseen conflict arises. For larger events that lock in a date on the school events calendar, your alternate plan requires having backup activities ready. In either case, communicate clearly to all participants that they must notify you immediately if any schedule conflicts arise. Establishing clear expectations can prevent some troubles, but inevitable frustrations like unexpected illness or uncooperative weather demand contingency plans.

I recruited three volunteer speakers for "The Hero in You." By doing so, I tripled the risk of encountering unexpected problems. Consequently, I prepared alternative activities to fill any of those three speakers' time slots. For Crusaders, I had a video about Joan of Arc queued to show a 15-minute segment. For Champions, I had the audio version of Michael Jordan reading his autobiography ready to play. And for Visionaries, I earmarked some pages of Cervantes's classic, *Don Quixote*, as well as some from Will Eisner's comic book style, children's version, *The Last Knight*, to read.

Completing Final Preparations

By this stage, you've chosen a program topic; determined learning objectives; set goals; planned activities; and chosen the audience, location, and time of the event. You are now ready to plan the program day.

Identify, Select, and Prepare Student and Parent Volunteers

Elementary school media specialists often have many regularly scheduled parent volunteers. You, however, will probably have to recruit assistants for major programs. Instead of seeking support only for the day of the event, line up volunteers to help before, during, and after the program. If you have parent volunteers, you probably found them by surveying parents at the beginning of the year. For special programs, return to the surveys you've kept on file and telephone parents who expressed interest in volunteering at special events. Also ask the PTA or PTO to support the program by finding volunteers for this one occasion. Regardless of how you recruit them, good volunteers significantly lessen your workload and your anxiety.

After securing helpers, conduct a meeting to assign volunteers specific responsibilities. Your main goal is to find the best person for each program task. In the process, you also must help volunteers become clear and comfortable with their job in the program. Therefore, during the meeting

- Establish a friendly yet businesslike rapport;
- Provide an overview of the upcoming program, including date and time;
- Build enthusiasm for the program throughout the meeting;
- Express clearly your vision of how the program day will evolve;
- Make certain all volunteers understand that they will work during the preparation stages as well as the day of the program;
- Explain which volunteer positions need filling;
- Tell volunteers that you value their input;
- Give volunteers an opportunity to choose what they want to do;
- Fill all volunteer positions; and
- Discuss the tasks required of each volunteer.

Before the day of the event, volunteers can

- Help with publicity (make posters, signs, and banners; write articles for newspaper);
- Research the topic;
- Help locate resources;
- Assist in developing book displays;
- Decorate the facility;
- Hang artwork;
- Help create enrichment activities to follow the program; or
- Help design interest centers.

On the day of, or during, the program, volunteers can

- Arrange furniture;
- Operate audiovisual equipment and computers;
- Serve as hosts and greet guests;
- Monitor traffic flow;
- Help with lighting; or
- Remind classes of assigned times to arrive at the program.

Publicize the Event

To be successful, an event must be advertised. As suggested previously, get backing from the principal and teachers early; their enthusiasm for a special event helps inspire students. (In most cases, students are the intended program audience, so direct all publicity toward them.)

Photo 3.1. For Teen Read Week, library media specialists at Palatine High School in Illinois advertised their "Take Time to Read" program in the auditorium showcase.

Publicity targeted to students can include posters, daily announcements, newsletters, and, if the school has one, marquee advertisements. Publicize the event in your school newspaper by asking a student to write an article about the program topic or inviting a student reporter to interview you. If publications exist at the district level, notify the administrative communications department about the upcoming event.

Get students involved in the advertising campaign by sponsoring poster contests. To fulfill part of their community service requirements, National Honor Society members can design invitations to send to parents, administrators, and community members.

One particularly creative media specialist in Florida, Robin Killingsworth, cleverly enlists student help in every facet of advertising. Robin sponsors a scholarship contest where students create an entire advertising portfolio and marketing plan that includes designing and distributing posters, invitations, and newsletters. With a little self-promotion, she enlisted the financial assistance of the administration and a local parent teacher organization to underwrite the scholarship, which has grown to $500. While providing students with hands-on experience and a financial reward, Robin gets all of her promotional material designed and marketed.

When planning an extravaganza, inform local newspapers or television stations. If you have never done so before, contact the communications department for your district or find out from your Campus Communicator (or onsite PR person) how to secure coverage of your event. If neither of these options works, ask a journalism teacher to take pictures during your event. Afterward, get students who appear in the pictures to sign release forms, then send the photos and a publicity sheet to the newspaper.

Remember that newspaper staffs work to strict deadlines and have many considerations to determine what is newsworthy. The timing of your event or even the number of articles they've recently published about your school or district may determine whether your submission is printed. Whatever their policies are, respect them. If they work into your plans, capitalize on them. If they do not work this time, just learning about them can help when you plan subsequent events.

Whether through television, newspapers, or even just letters to parents, let community members know what your media center is offering. It reflects well on you and your school.

Prepare Students and Teachers for the Event

Your publicity blitz should also target teachers. Prior to many programs, teachers should provide students with background information on the topic. For example, weeks before her guest author arrived for a program, media specialist Greta Lawry gave junior English teachers sets of paperback books by the author. In return, those teachers added that author's name to the list from which students selected their biographical research topics. Before a class attended the program, students who chose that author for their research assignment presented a mini-lesson in class about that author's life and works.

All this preparation helped students and teachers anticipate her program. Additionally, it made an often stale assignment—the required author research paper—come alive, especially for students who think that only dull books by dead authors become required reading. Clearly, with additional information offered through direct instruction, students can be richly prepared for a program.

Greta included an impressive touch in her author programs. She purchased a plaque listing the name of each guest author and the date of his or her visit. Over time, the plaque— a Who's Who of YA authors—became fine publicity when guests visited her media center. (Many YA authors' Web sites are listed in Chapter 6.)

Schedule Classes

If your program targets classes where nearly every student is in one grade level, scheduling is relatively simple. When planning programs for multiple grades, you must take into account all affected schedules, including music, athletics, vocational, co-op, independent studies, and lunch. Whatever your target audience, involve teachers in the scheduling process from the beginning. Teachers tend to be more flexible if they have been apprised of program plans from the start. Their support and cooperation are essential to scheduling your event.

Different types of programs often influence scheduling:

- If the program is a display or exhibit, teachers may sign up to bring classes to the media center. When appropriate, let teachers bring classes at their convenience.
- If the program is an interest center, schedule classes to participate in the center. Or allow teachers to send small groups or individual students to the media center with a pass.
- If the program is a demonstration or presentation by a guest speaker, classes or select groups must attend at your designated time.

Whatever schedule you set, remind teachers about it up to the very morning of the event:

- Mention the program schedule at several faculty meetings before the event.
- Share the schedule with teachers at club or organization meetings.
- Send out reminders on attractive flyers.
- Post reminders in the teachers' lounge.
- Enlist volunteers to help remind teachers about the schedule.
- Make an announcement over the intercom the day before, and the day of, the event.

Arranging the Facility

An attractive facility adds vitality and sets the tone for your program. Enhance program success by decorating, arranging furniture, providing for traffic flow, and using technology.

Decorate

Put up attractive bulletin boards well before the event and leave them up during the program to enhance the atmosphere. Display books and objects related to the event. Choose decorations (balloons, memorabilia, student art) that set your desired tone. Let students participate by making and displaying decorations. They can make posters, banners, or art to hang on walls or from the ceiling. Display their written work as well. Mount essays and creative writing assignments on colorful backgrounds and hang them in a prominent place. Frequently, you can plan your decorating strategies with student and parent volunteers, then let them decorate.

For my Heroes unit, I discovered that several simple additions to my wall decorations transformed them from ordinary pictures into eye-catching displays. Lining the walls with ALA's celebrity "Read" posters barely enhanced the facility. But adding a little memorabilia made for engaging surroundings. On the ledge beneath each poster, I placed items related to the celebrity pictured. For example, under Oprah Winfrey's picture I placed a cardboard cutout of an Emmy award, a copy of *O* magazine, newspaper clippings about her generosity, and an enlargement of a check (which I created myself) for $10,000,000, made out (theoretically) by Oprah to a charitable organization. Under Shaquille O'Neill, I placed a basketball, a trading card on which he appears, a number 34 Los Angeles Lakers jersey, and a pair of size 22 basketball shoes donated by a local specialty men's store.

I also displayed near the pictures not only copies of the book the celebrities were holding but also books related to them or their professions. For example, for Oprah I had several "Oprah Book Club" titles; her exercise book, *Make the Connection*; copies of *The Color Purple* and *Beloved*, which were made into movies she starred in and/or produced; and several volumes of poetry by her friend and mentor, Maya Angelou.

Finally, while perusing a catalog from the store, Successories, I was inspired to find quotations from or about celebrities that addressed heroism. Onto each poster I taped the quotation, which students had typed in a unique font and laminated over different colored paper for me. Although the posters alone are so common that students might not even have noticed them, the unique items, especially Shaq's huge shoes, drew students to the displays and brought them back to check out books.

Arrange Furniture and Seating

If possible, arrange the furniture the day before your program. If not, draw a diagram of the room arrangement so volunteers can quickly set up the facility on the day of the event. To arrange furniture and accommodate seating, consider the following questions:

- Which volunteer is in charge of setting up the facility?
- Who will help arrange the furniture?
- Where should you place furniture being used for the program?
- Where should you place furniture not being used for the program?
- Where will the speaker stand?
- Will the speaker need a microphone?
- Will the speaker need a projection screen?
- Does the speaker have any special needs regarding seating arrangements or speaker podium?

- How many students and guests will attend?
- Where will the students sit?
- Should classes sit together?
- Does your seating arrangement give all students an unobstructed view of the presenters?
- Where can you, teachers, and adult volunteers sit (or stand) so you all can monitor student behavior with minimal interruption to the speaker?
- Where will special guests (administrators, community members) sit?
- Do presenters require a place to sit?
- Who will help put the furniture back in order following the program?

Provide for Traffic Flow

Programs for smaller groups seldom create traffic flow problems. Large events demand some creative planning to get students in and out of the facility expeditiously. To manage traffic flow, consider the following questions:

- When do I want students to arrive?
- Can all students arrive at once, or do I need to scatter arrival times?
- If I scatter arrival times, how will I notify teachers that it is time for them to bring classes? (I call? Volunteers call? Volunteers go to classes and escort students?)
- In what order should classes arrive?
- How much time will students need to be seated and to settle down?
- At what time should all students be seated and ready for the program?
- Do some students have special needs or considerations that must be addressed in advance? (For example, will students with physical challenges need to leave early?)
- Are a sufficient number of volunteers or student aides available to help supervise the traffic flow?

Use Technology Support

Some programs may depend entirely on technology. For example, showing the video, *White Squall,* on a separate day prior to "The Hero in You" made it a form of programming. Usually, technology supports other program formats. When you teach a concept using *PowerPoint* or a guest speaker uses an overhead projector or microphone to share information, technology is support.

Well before the day of your program, determine what equipment your guest presenters need. As a safeguard, give presenters a copy of your district copyright adherence policy. When you know exactly what equipment everyone needs, gather (or order) all equipment and software ahead of time. In some cases, technology materials must be scheduled weeks in advance.

When using multimedia, ask yourself the following questions:

- What equipment do presenters need?
- Will presenters bring their own equipment?
- Is my requested equipment in good working order?
- What software do presenters require?
- Do they want a podium or table and chair?
- Do the participants need a dryboard, easel, or chart?
- Where should I place the equipment?
- Will the equipment have to be moved during the program?
- Do participants know how to work the equipment?
- Do they need someone to operate it for them?
- Who will take care of lighting?
- Do I have backup equipment, extension cords, and extra bulbs available and handy?

Set up audiovisual equipment, including computers, microphones, and software support, the day before the event. Test it to make certain it works properly. Check focus and sound levels from all areas in the facility where equipment will be used. Ensure that the screen, if one is needed, is positioned for optimal viewing wherever participants may be seated. Just before students arrive, test everything once more.

If presenters want to operate the equipment themselves, let them test the equipment so they feel comfortable using it. If they request a volunteer's assistance, be sure the volunteer is ready and knows what support the presenter needs. Address these concerns and do all last minute troubleshooting before students arrive.

Executing the Program

For events requiring one or more speakers, tend to the following details on the program day:

- Remind teachers and students of program times and their seating times.
- Remind volunteers about the times and scheduling.
- Review with the volunteers their assigned tasks.
- Complete final seating arrangements.
- Check the environment: temperature, lighting, and ventilation.
- Make certain the speakers' requests have been met before they arrive.
- Greet the speakers.
- Make sure they are comfortable with the equipment, room arrangement, program agenda, and schedule.
- Review with the speakers the importance of staying on the time schedule (if it's helpful, provide a signal to end the presentation).
- Spend some time after the program with the guests (coffee, lunch, a short visit).

Present the Program

Although others share the responsibilities for your program, its success depends on you. To ensure that it is executed precisely and professionally, follow these steps:

1. Begin at the scheduled time.

2. Welcome patrons and provide a brief introduction to the program topic.

3. Acknowledge everyone who contributed to the program.

4. Remind students of expectations for behavior and participation (for example, when during the program it is appropriate for them to ask questions).

5. Introduce the guest speaker.

6. Monitor students during the presentation.

7. Devise a subtle way of signaling to the speakers when their time is nearly over.

8. When each speaker has finished, thank him or her for the presentation.

9. At the end, thank everyone for attending.

10. With the help of your volunteers, instruct students and teachers how and when they should leave the facility.

Follow Through After the Event

Once the event is over, your program is not complete without appropriate reinforcement. To ensure that students get the most out of the program, provide follow-up activities. In some way, these activities must review or extend information shared during the program. The following options for media specialists and teachers will provide student enrichment.

- Consider a follow-up event or demonstration on the same topic.
- Make books on related topics available for checkout.
- Make media on related topics available to teachers.
- Provide enrichment activities in the school library media center.
- Compile a Webography on your program topic and display it near the computers.
- Encourage and suggest individual or classroom activities.
- Give both students and teachers bibliographies of related student resources.
- Give teachers a bibliography of related professional materials.
- Request feedback from the students and teachers about the program. (see Chapter 7)

Following Your Program Checklist

In programming, there is much to consider and do. Following a structured checklist (see Figure 3.1) can help you organize your work and complete all necessary tasks for planning, presenting, and assessing your program.

PROGRAM CHECKLIST

Several Months Prior to Event
_____ Decide theme/topic
_____ Develop objectives
_____ Identify available resources

One Month Prior to Event
_____ Obtain permission from administration
_____ Select participants
_____ Select materials
_____ Identify audience, date, and time
_____ Contact participants
_____ Begin publicizing event
_____ Develop contingency plans:
_____ Alternate dates
_____ Alternate activities
_____ Alternate speakers

One to Two Weeks Prior to Event
_____ Schedule volunteers
_____ Determine seating arrangements
_____ Determine traffic flow
_____ Give teachers schedule of event
_____ At faculty meeting, discuss event (problems, schedules, etc.)

Day Prior to Event
_____ Prepare seating arrangement
_____ Prepare audiovisual equipment
_____ Arrange decorations, displays, and exhibits
_____ Remind volunteers and participants of time
_____ Remind teachers of schedule

Day of Event
_____ Do last minute check of facility:
_____ Room temperature
_____ Lighting
_____ Room arrangement
_____ Audiovisual equipment and cords
_____ Speaker podium
_____ Seating arrangement
_____ Review individual duties with volunteers
_____ Greet speakers

After the Event
_____ Do informal evaluation
_____ Do formal evaluation
_____ Send letters of appreciation to participants
_____ Analyze program

Figure 3.1. Checklist for successful programs.

Conclusion

If developing a program seems as overwhelming as it is exciting, start small. Limit your theme, your audience, and your format. Invite one speaker to present to a single class. Even simpler, create an interest center around an intriguing theme. Consider renting (for a nominal fee) a pre-designed display from a museum or cultural organization. (See the list in Chapter 4.) Create an interactive bulletin board or display. From there, let your programs grow. With inspiration from initial successes, you will soon coordinate multifaceted programs that make lasting impressions.

Chapter 4

How to Identify and Locate Resources

Satisfied with my "Read" displays, I began gathering resources for the event itself. For the Crusaders segment, I wanted to address history, religion, and women. A resource person came immediately to mind for both history and women. Our superintendent of schools was the first woman to hold that position in the nearly 100-year history of my district. Thinking about this achievement, I realized that women had prominent positions throughout the district. The associate superintendent, the principals of two high schools, even the administrator who oversaw all the district libraries, all were female.

Because I had always been one of the few men on the English faculty and I'm the district's only male librarian, that fact didn't initially strike me as unique. But at a recent convention, a female publisher despaired about being one of few women to hold a top position at a major publishing house. "I only have this job," she grimaced, "because the economy is good. If the market were tighter, my job would have been given to a man." If her comment was eye opening to me, imagine what it would mean to teen patrons who may not appreciate what a milestone it was for my superintendent to attain her position. She became my first scheduled speaker.

In today's global society, you have access to a plethora of resource people and materials. Your challenge, then, is not locating resources but selecting the guests and materials that best support your programs.

Identifying Resources

Initially, your resource options may seem vague or overwhelmingly broad. But as you search, you will quickly discover what types or resources exist, who has them, and when they are available.

Educational Resources

Before searching, become familiar with the many different types of educational resources that support programming. As you search, you may discover resources not mentioned below. Knowing about the major resource options described in this section can give you a clear vision for the kind of program support to pursue.

Books

Books are integral to all school library media programs. Sometimes a book or books will be the program topic. Even if your event focuses on developing a skill, such as learning some new technology, include books. Have them handy for introducing information before and during the program and make them available after the program to extend learning. Because our primary goal as educators is to encourage lifelong readers, make books a central component of any program.

After gathering all book resources from your media center, search for more from other media specialists in your district. If you belong to a professional online networking organization (California, Florida, and Texas have prominent ones), you can collect resources state-wide. Once you begin developing long-term visions for future programs, you may budget for and order resources to have on hand when you are ready to plan the event.

Professional Materials

When gathering resources for programs, search your campus or district professional collection. Many of these books and journals explore education theory and share creative classroom activities. In them you may find worthwhile information to supplement programs for students or professional growth activities to use for programs directed to faculty.

Remember, teachers may have resources in their departments that you would not normally keep in your media center. Physical education equipment, history games, lab equipment, and class sets of novels could supplement a program in their respective subject areas.

Audiovisual Materials

Like any lesson, a program should meet the needs of visual, auditory, and kinesthetic learners. Eye-catching visuals, appealing graphics, and appropriate audio elements hold students' attention and enhance learning. After deciding what audiovisual (AV) materials to incorporate into your program, begin gathering resources from your own collection. Videos, books on tape, and CD-ROMs that you initially ordered for classroom use may meet your program needs. As suggested previously, expand your search incrementally. Ask department chairpersons if they have resources you need. If you have a regional distribution center that lends AV materials, check their catalog or Web site and order what you want well before the program. Preview the work to determine its quality and decide what parts you will include in the program. Don't risk not having the material on your program date. Better to get it early and request an extension than to discover that your well-timed order was never filled.

Also, consider creating AV materials. Attractive overheads complement your programs. Because they combine information, visual movement, and sound effects, *PowerPoint* presentations are outstanding teaching tools. Sometimes filming your own video personalizes the learning for students, especially if some have contributed to the effort. For example, when a media specialist in Oklahoma could not find a video that succinctly explained tools of early Native Americans, she and some students videotaped a demonstration with props and artifacts she had collected.

Once you determine your AV needs, set aside or reserve equipment. You probably have much of what you need already. Gather it together and check it out to yourself. You don't want an assistant or volunteer unknowingly issuing the equipment to a teacher just as you are prepared to use it. If a teacher already has equipment you want for your program, arrange early to get it back, or negotiate a plan to have a volunteer retrieve and return it.

More expensive equipment, such as an LCD projector, may be harder to acquire. Some districts purchase one such item, then make it available to all campuses, or limit its use to the administrative offices. Get an up-to-date list of your district's AV equipment and the ordering policy. Sometimes, waiting lists make it impossible to secure the equipment you want unless you've requested it several months in advance.

Check with other school library media specialists. Some colleagues work closely together, each agreeing to order different AV materials and share them among campuses. Others have a central budget controlled by an administrative coordinator. At the very least, suggest that all media specialists in your district list the AV equipment they have and are willing to share, then distribute those lists at the next meeting. Having immediate access to this list can save much time as you gather program resources.

Teacher- and Student-Made Resources

As an educator, you probably create some support material from scratch. Making your own program resources, alone or with teachers and students, can benefit everyone. It is usually economical for you. It can offer teachers a new focus for a familiar lesson. It can provide students with a creative activity and a chance to contribute to a major event. For example, instead of requiring individual students to write reports, a U.S. history teacher introduced his students to jackdaws and allowed groups of students to compile them for his Civil War unit. They gave their best projects to the media specialist, who displayed them in the library media center.

Jackdaws

A jackdaw is a compilation of materials kept in a portfolio. Whether teacher-made or commercially produced, they can contain reproductions of historical documents, maps, photos, and other interesting educational materials that bring to life a period of history or literary work. Jackdaws may be paired with information books, biographies, or historical fiction.

To support a program for American literature students, I created a jackdaw on *The Great Gatsby* that contained a diagram of East and West Egg, the article accusing Jordan Baker of cheating at a golf tournament, Daisy's tub-soaked letter from Gatsby, the "schedule" and list of "general resolves" that Gatsby's father brought to the funeral, and even Meyer Wolfsheim's molar cufflinks. Except for buying the binder and protector sheets to hold the materials, I spent no money by making everything myself. I drew the diagram; composed the article; wrote, soaked, and dried the letter; typed Gatsby's schedules and resolves; and even made the cufflinks by hot gluing some fake teeth from a dental display onto old cufflinks I had at home. It was a fun and simple project that made my program memorable.

Besides being attractive and useful, jackdaws are easy to store. Although some media specialists keep jackdaws only for their programs and displays, others catalog them and allow teachers and students to check them out for classroom use. When planning a program for teachers, note that "Creating Jackdaws" is an excellent topic. Jackdaws are simple to compile, versatile, and still unfamiliar to many teachers.

Student Art

As decoration and program support, student art can significantly enhance your media center. Collaborating with art teachers, one media specialist enhanced her facility for an entire school year. She developed a different theme for each of seven months, then asked art teachers to assign art projects relating to the theme. On their designated month, students brought completed art to the school library media center and built displays of their work themselves. Some theme suggestions are listed in Figure 4.1.

October	Scenes from a Haunted House
November	If the Pilgrims Landed on Mars
December	A Multicultural Christmas
January	The Bleak Midwinter
February	If Mount Rushmore Were Carved Today
March	Original Posters for Oscar-Nominated Films
April	A Rainy Afternoon

Figure 4.1. Art program themes.

Keep in mind that students often enjoy creating art in unique formats, including manipulatives, jackdaws, and even three-dimensional examples of monthly art projects (e.g., clay versions of Mount Rushmore were especially impressive).

Student Projects

You may already have classes displaying student projects in the school library media center. At different times in my own facility, I have had period costumes (a combined effort from the home economics and drama classes); pyramids and Aztec ruins (compliments of the world history classes); and (thanks to consistent contributions from the English department) models of guillotines from *A Tale of Two Cities*, Huck Finn's raft, and even the concentration camp from *One Day in the Life of Ivan Denisovich*.

While adding character to the school library media center and allowing students to display their work, projects also enhance programming. With students' permission, projects may be stored and used for future programs. Some library media specialists find students to create projects for upcoming programs. Both strategies can work. Sometimes projects inspire program ideas. At other times, program planning involves allowing students to contribute projects that support the program goals.

Photo 4.1. Student projects, like these models of the Empire State Building and the Chrysler Building displayed at T. L. Hanna High School in Anderson, South Carolina, provide dramatic program support.

Interactive Bulletin Boards

Interactive bulletin boards are usually three-dimensional displays that attract patrons and encourage independent learning. They usually have three standard components: an intriguing title, information that ties in with current learning, and an interactive game or puzzle that requires students to use their new knowledge.

Such bulletin boards can be used in all disciplines. For a language arts program, one media specialist entitled her board, "Whose Line Was It, Anyway?" and presented short biographical information beneath pictures of a few key poets. Then she cut out lines from different poems unique to each author, mounted and laminated them, and set them in the book tray beneath her bulletin board. The interactive game required students to place each line of poetry beside the author who, based upon the information provided, must have written that line. Clues within lines related to themes (death, nature), details (blindness, poverty), style (humorous, gothic), and diction (seventeenth-century British, contemporary African-American). Once placed down the center of the board beside the authors' pictures, the lines formed an original, humorously anachronistic poem that piqued student interest and encouraged them to mix and match other works from their textbook for more comic creations.

Combining geography and science, another media specialist hung different rock samples from strings attached to a world map. Under each continent she placed a small, clear plastic cup. Using sidebar information that described rock formations around the world, students were invited to place each rock sample in the correct cup. To check their accuracy, they lifted the one country outlined in red on each continent. Under it was a picture and the name of the correct rock.

Manipulatives

Manipulatives are to high school media centers what puppets are to elementary libraries. Whereas many popular programs for elementary students involve using puppets, high school students generally find them too juvenile. However, especially for kinesthetic learners, manipulatives prove the perfect hands-on medium for interactive learning.

Manipulatives are any three-dimensional objects that (as the name implies) can be manipulated manually for multisensory learning. For example, an architectural scale model of a building that is merely constructed and painted is not a manipulative. But one that has working doors and windows and is constructed from samples of the actual materials of the building (glass, adobe, stone, cement), which students can feel first-hand, is. Although some teachers consider plastic three-dimensional geometric figures manipulatives for classroom use, true manipulatives allow students to construct and re-create shapes, such as circles that can be stretched into ovals or squares that can be shifted into rectangles.

Such geometric figures and architectural scale models are examples of commercially designed manipulatives that can be purchased or rented. More common and cost-effective are student- and teacher-made manipulatives. The English or drama department might build a scale model of the Globe Theater with props and working trap doors. For experiments, the science department could construct a maze with moveable panels.

Such manipulatives are commonly used for demonstration purposes during a program, but they are especially inviting to students when left on display after programs are completed. Place them close enough to the circulation desk so you can monitor their use, but far enough away so students who genuinely want to experiment with them and learn independently can feel free to do so.

Locating Resources

Now that you know many of the resources that support programming, your search will indicate who has them and when they are available. Set parameters for your search by answering the following three questions:

1. What do I want?

2. What can I afford?

3. When do I need it?

Your answers narrow your search and give it direction.

Your Campus

You are surrounded by outstanding program support every day at work. Materials in your own inventory may be precisely what you need. Or you may search other areas of your campus to find people and materials for great programming.

Your School Library Media Center

Begin gathering resources from your library media center. Often books and materials in your collection inspire your program ideas or clarify your program focus. Because you know your collection, finding books and materials should be simple. What you have on hand determines how deep and extensive your subsequent search must be.

Classrooms and Offices

After exhausting all possibilities from your media center, expand your search incrementally. A little investigating may reveal that colleagues on your campus have expertise or collections appropriate for your program. A teacher or administrator may be your best choice for guest speaker. Why go through the process of finding, interviewing, and inviting an unfamiliar speaker from the community when many of your colleagues, who relate to teens for a living and will be on campus anyway, could enthusiastically share their knowledge about a favorite topic?

Colleagues also may share relevant support material from their own departments or from their personal collections. For example, one library media specialist in Houston found enough materials on Texas history in the social studies department closet to decorate her entire facility for an event. In my school, a program on inventions and innovations really came alive thanks to a colleague's willingness to share her personal collection of *Titanic* memorabilia. As a special treat, she was able to get us a copy of one of Robert Ballard's books, *Lost Liners: From the Titanic to the Andrea Doria,* autographed by the underwater explorer himself.

Finally, class sets of novels from the language arts department can support programs. Depending on the nature and target audience of the program, sometimes having students read excerpts aloud from an author's work varies your program and encourages active participation.

Your District

To obtain more resources at no cost, tap other areas of your district beyond your campus. Even though site-based management allots separate budget money to each school, the district administrative offices still have more financial resources than even the largest campuses. Although they may not be able to supplement your program financially, they may have expensive equipment that you cannot obtain otherwise. Just as faculty and staff in your building can be great resource possibilities, so too can administrators, teachers, and other media specialists throughout your district.

Administrative Offices

Your district administrative offices have human and materials resources that can significantly improve your program quality. Often budget restrictions may prevent you from ordering some dynamic equipment available through the district communications department. Although some individual library media centers have their own broadcasting equipment or even facility, most do not. But your administration might. Find out who coordinates district-wide inservice events or find your district PR representative. Either of those staff members may have digital cameras, recording and projection equipment, and computer hardware and software that can enable you to present larger, more sophisticated programs.

Professional Libraries

To find available professional resources, visit your district's professional library, if you are fortunate enough to have one. Such libraries (usually in teacher centers) often have resources that support programming. Many district libraries issue support materials such as films and computer software. A few also offer research services that locate professional articles on your topic, identify information about authors, guide Internet searches, or secure appointments from available speakers. Even if they cannot make the arrangements for you, they may have a community resources file that includes possible speakers.

Other School Library Media Centers

You are probably already in close contact with other high school media specialists in your district. Establish a routine of informing each other about new resources by listing good program ideas and support material that you're willing to share. Ask your colleagues to do the same. If you don't already alternate campuses for your regular meetings, start. While visiting another media center, ask for a tour, especially of the storage, periodical, and AV rooms. You may be inspired by something that your colleagues never even thought to mention.

Realize that colleagues at elementary and middle school media centers may also have materials worth acquiring. Their facilities are usually brimming with kits, games, decorations, and manipulatives that may work into a program. Although you are not likely to have your patrons play a game meant for elementary students, you might use game pieces or parts of kits to create your own activities.

Other media specialists at any level may maintain diverse, full, and current community resources files. When accessing such a treasure, discuss programming ideas and resources with the other media specialists. If you already have a community resources file of your own, add to it with materials from your colleagues. If you do not, you will develop one as you begin exploring the resources available throughout your community.

Community Resources

Your program choices often reflect the beliefs, attitudes, and dreams of your students and their community. Until recently, smaller communities might draw from rich local archives and big cities had more high tech and diverse resource possibilities. With global communication and the Internet, however, populations at both extremes are now converging. For my programs, I have borrowed sophisticated software that my budget could never have accommodated. Because my school has existed for so long, I can share historical resources (books long out-of-print, vertical file materials, even outdated equipment and media material kept for its historic appeal) with other media specialists.

Finding resources requires knowing what people, places, institutions, businesses, organizations and clubs, government agencies, and special holidays and events exist in a community. Some programs evolve entirely around a single community resource, such as a guest speaker or unique display. To support a school-wide campaign against violence, a media specialist in Wyoming hosted a program about school safety presented entirely by local peace officers. Other programs may require only supplemental support from the community. One media specialist presented a program called "Careers in Health Care." Afterward, she distributed pamphlets collected from local doctor's offices, hospitals, rehabilitation centers, and hospices.

For this part of your search especially, be systematic. Chart a course for identifying and locating resources. Decide what you want, then list logical providers. Knowing budget, time, and space parameters will also help you decide what resources to pursue. Figure 4.2 lists resources available in most communities. Beyond these suggestions, consider resources unique to your community because of local traditions and industry.

Resource People

Library media specialists seldom need to search hard for community members eager to share their expertise. Community members may come to you to share their unique talents. More often you will hear about them through others or read about them in local news features. Staying alert to extraordinary and even mildly interesting news items that you come across daily can lead you to program participants.

Begin looking in your own school. Students and teachers have special skills, interests, or achievements that program participants might enjoy. If your campus has a social committee, they have probably surveyed teachers about hobbies, collections, and travel experiences. If not, suggest that someone start a committee. Or send out a get-acquainted survey at the beginning of the year asking teachers to list hobbies that they might like to share with students some time. Common hobbies such as gardening or painting can enhance some programs as much as pastimes like birding or collecting antique toys.

Because other media specialists in your district may be investigating similar information at their schools, plan sharing time during a meeting to let each other know about unique human resources at every campus. Such a session allowed me to volunteer for a program about reading hosted by an elementary library media specialist and to share some of my fiction during a program for the creative writing class at another high school.

Consider professionals in the community (including parents) as possible speakers for programs. Writers, artists, doctors, architects, attorneys, pilots, scientists, and engineers are frequently invited to career days and may be receptive to speaking at other special programs. Government office holders and employees of institutions, businesses, and government agencies are usually top level contacts. Bright, active volunteers and retired persons can provide enrichment on various topics. Members of local clubs and organizations or retirees who participate in specialized groups related to their former professions are wellsprings of information. For help in finding resources, check resources lists at the public library.

Locating Resources

Type of Resource	Sources
Resource people	Questionnaire PTA or PTO Faculty recommendations Public library
Interesting places	Chamber of Commerce City guides Internet (see Chapter 6)
Institutions	Telephone directory Internet (see Chapter 6) Teacher/parent recommendations
Business and industry	Telephone directory Chamber of Commerce Internet (see Chapter 6) Teacher/parent recommendations
Clubs and organizations	Chamber of Commerce Directories Internet (see Chapter 6) Teacher/parent recommendation
Government agencies	Internet (see Chapter 6) Telephone directory
Holidays and special events	Chamber of Commerce News media
Professional materials	Selection aids (see Chapter 6)
Displays and exhibits	Museums, businesses, institutions, organizations Media resources (magazines, television) Internet (see Chapter 6) Other libraries

Figure 4.2. Resources and places to locate them.

Interesting Places

Special places in your community are so easy to take for granted, you may overlook them when considering resources. These sites may include tourist attractions, historic sights, government buildings, landmarks, parks, gardens, fountains, and even shopping malls. Students frequently take field trips to places that could also enrich media programs by providing brochures, pamphlets, and speakers.

Institutions

When seeking community resources, note that institutions have materials or resource people related to the secondary curriculum and student interests. By targeting the right institution for your program, you can secure most of the materials or presenters you need with one telephone call. Figure 4.3 presents examples of institutions that frequently support programs in high schools along with program titles that have worked well for media specialists.

Institutions	Program Titles
Library	Internet Search Training
University	New Technology for Educators (professor presents program to faculty)
Zoo	Preserving Wildlife
Museum	Soup, Soup, Soup, Soup (the "Pop" psychology of Andy Warhol)
Hospital	Sirens, Speed, and Stress (An EMT presents information on his career)
Bank	Save for Your Future Now

Figure 4.3. Examples of institutions and program titles.

Public Libraries

What you don't find in your own media center or cannot obtain through district interlibrary loan you may find at the public library. As part of their outreach programs, county and city libraries frequently use programming to teach concepts or to increase public awareness of their facility. Although these librarians more frequently present programs for children than for teens, they can still share great ideas and resources to support your programming efforts. Consider joining a "Friends of the Public Library" organization (they have different names in different parts of the country) to continually be apprised of their programs and new PR strategies for attracting patrons.

Colleges and Universities

Colleges and universities are especially helpful for programs directed at high school audiences. As the trend toward offering advanced placement and early college credit courses increases, think about offering a program for students and parents on this topic. Invite counselors to share information about how credits are earned, what extra responsibilities will be required in this curriculum, and how these credits affect points toward graduation. These programs will be well attended because the topic has immediate relevance. A comfortable forum for sharing ideas can serve both parents and students well.

Furthermore, such programs establish a partnership between you and the counselors, an opportunity that presents itself less frequently than cooperative sessions with other teachers.

More tangential programs can be discovered through colleges and universities as well. Contact the public relations department of local universities, or the fine arts or language arts departments directly, to discover what guest authors, art exhibits, or programs they open to young patrons. Don't just pass the information on to teachers as possible field trip opportunities. Instead, offer correlating events on campus to pique student interest and expand their knowledge before they attend the university event. During lunch, read works by an author who will soon visit the university. Create a learning center on artistic movements covered in upcoming exhibits. Fun and educational mini-lessons related to the university's program empower students to be informed, active learners on their field trip.

Every upcoming field trip is a program opportunity. When you hear announcements about upcoming trips or see them listed on school calendars, ask sponsoring teachers to give a mini-program that prepares students for the trip. Often, the best teachers coordinate field trips with lessons they're either beginning or have just finished in the classroom. While students are engaged in classroom learning, you can support their lesson by hosting a program on a related topic. If nothing else, at the very least ask teachers to bring back materials from the trip so you can offer them to library patrons. Items may include interactive programs from the science museum, sample demos from the local radio station, or Webographies of art and artists from the fine arts museum.

Even if no one plans a field trip to these facilities, you can bring part of an institution to your campus. A professor of architecture in Chicago not only narrates guided river tours through downtown, but she also travels to schools with a jackdaw containing graphics, blueprints, and photographs of the city's skyscrapers to host programs. Institutions of all types have employees and volunteers willing to come to your campus to guide students through riveting educational experiences.

Vocational Campuses and Specialized Schools

Vocational classes, which may not use the library media center as often as core subject areas, offer a wellspring of resource opportunities. Health occupation classes visit hospitals for everything from experiencing a few hours in an emergency room to observing open heart surgery. Consider vocational classes—electronics, cosmetology, metal trades, auto paint and body—as potential gold mines of resources and program ideas.

Some students choose vocational training because they have neither the inclination nor the income to pursue higher education. These students especially could benefit from programs centering around specific trades. Programs with hands-on activities where students create a product can be very meaningful. Designing computer-generated T-shirt decals or compiling modeling portfolios are only two ideas that students could use to sharpen their skills or to find a job.

For programs like these, specialized schools may be able to contribute both human and material resources. A representative from a local business school told me recently how disheartening it is to attend college and career night at high school campuses. Because her school is small, she is usually relegated to a little table sandwiched between a canopy-covered area for one ivy league school and a three-table spread from a state university. This type of forum can be defeating to small specialty schools, even well-respected ones. However, a program in the library resource center can help teens recognize that not all students who do not attend four-year colleges are destined to serve fast food or work assembly lines.

In cities large and small you can find beauty schools, automotive training centers, secretarial and legal assistant programs, even culinary and fine arts academies. Some of these schools present special motivational programs as a way of introducing themselves to students. In my school, a local business training center schedules talks on listening skills, goal setting, and learning styles through English classes. Such presentations need not cut into classroom instruction time. Host them in the library media center.

Schedule such presentations on pep rally days if attending the pep rally is optional, or during review week if your school allows some students to be exempted from taking exams. That way, students who don't want to attend the pep rally or who don't need the review have a productive alternative activity. With optional participation, students who attend are likely to be more interested and cooperative. By suggesting that a company switch its presentation to your facility, you can offer a custom-made program that only requires you to do a little scheduling and student monitoring.

Business and Industry

As independent studies courses become more common across the nation, alliances between schools and businesses grow deeper and richer. Previously only vocational education students combined class work with on-the-job training. Now independent studies programs allow the most academically astute students to be mentored by exceptional achievers in the business world.

When I was a classroom teacher, I spearheaded the independent studies program at my high school. Even in its infancy, the program had astounding results. One student found as his mentor a famous Houston attorney. Once a week, the student worked at his mentor's downtown law firm. Within weeks, he went from helping the clerk file and the legal assistant research to actually observing some meetings with associates and clients.

As part of this program, students are required to complete a major project demonstrating what they have learned. The evening when students share their achievements is as impressive as regional science fairs. Attendees include teachers, the mentors, parents, board members, and administrators. And where is this extravaganza usually held?—in the school library media center.

If your school already has such a program in place and participants use your facility for demonstration night, simply extending the learning makes it another program for which you can take credit. Invite students to display their work for a few days before the big event or leave it afterward for classes to peruse during the school day. Knowing the topics beforehand allows you to pull resources (reference books, vocational texts, biographies of people in related professions) or help advertise the event. Students might even earn extra credit points by repeating their event demonstration to classes who might appreciate their work.

Even if no such program exists in your district, you can still get companies to participate. To fulfill community service responsibilities, businesses frequently collaborate with area schools to help students learn about different professions. When approached, most companies are pleased to help young people learn about their business or provide resources for programs. Predictably, such generosity is only part altruism. The success of any business depends on good PR. Supporting the schools impresses administrators, school board members (who are usually businesspersons in the community), and parents. Furthermore, by sponsoring school events, a company's name becomes recognizable to teen consumers. While helping you, they are employing one of the most cost-effective forms of advertising.

Most large businesses have huge PR departments whose representatives welcome the opportunity to work with library media specialists. Before contacting any businesses, know your district's policies about working with them. Especially stay in tune with any contracts your district has that restrict doing business with certain competitors. For example, many districts sign contracts with specific copy machine corporations or soft drink vendors that require the schools to use only their products. Such deals often come with multimillion dollar advances that districts could lose if someone inadvertently violates the contract. Although PR persons should know whether their company is commissioned to do business with your district, they may not. Responsibility for that knowledge lies with you.

Fortunately, your administration offices probably have a list of businesses with whom they have good relations. Start with that list to secure guest speakers, financial backers, or valuable program resources. Other library media specialists in your district could also recommend companies that have been supportive or warn you about companies that have reneged on promises. Finally, ask the counselors which local businesses support the schools by participating in career events or offering scholarships. Local businesses that give scholarships often have long-term visions to help students become successful. That spirit of encouragement translates into great interactions and generous support in ways beyond financial donations.

Like the specialty school mentioned in the previous section, some businesses have programs already prepared for presenting at schools. Figure 4.4 lists a few businesses and the topics they shared in various schools.

Businesses/Companies	Program Titles
Bookstore	Murder by the Book
Boutique	What Color and Season Are You?
Gym	Muscle Up to Fitness
Radio station	So You Wanna Be a D. J.?
Restaurant	Fine Dining: The World Beyond Pizza and Tacos
Travel agency	Spring Break Trips That Won't Break You

Figure 4.4. Examples of businesses and program titles.

Besides the companies listed in Figure 4.4, other professions have much to offer teens. Some businesses worth contacting are the following:

Airlines	Doctors' offices	Musical equipment stores
Architectural firms	Drug stores	Pet shops
Automobile dealers	Electric companies	Police and security companies
Banks	Ethnic food stores	Radio stations
Beauty salons	Gas companies	Sporting goods stores
Boat and yacht businesses	Interior design firms	Stock brokers
Building supply stores	Jewelers	Telephone companies
Cable companies	Landscaping businesses	Theaters
Cinemas	Law firms	Video stores
Computer stores	Limousine services	Vitamin and nutrition stores
Concert promoters	Marketing companies	Whole food stores
Dentists' offices	Motorcycle shops	
Department stores	Music stores	

Clubs and Organizations

Members of major clubs and organizations often love to share their expertise with interested young people. Note that special interest clubs and organizations can also offer program support. For example, when contacting sports clubs, standard sports such as volleyball, skiing, tennis, swimming, and soccer may come to mind immediately. But realize that special interest sports including skateboarding, surfing, and even river rafting can also supply great resources.

Don't rule out major sports organizations. Although securing their support usually requires a personal connection, you would be surprised to discover how many high school coaches either played or worked for these organizations. If you cannot find connections, redirect your search to amateur players and coaches. Many amateurs are passionate about their favorite pastime and are therefore thrilled to share their knowledge with students. Their experience and zeal make amateur athletes among the most popular and effective program presenters.

Cultural arts organizations have performing artists such as dancers, thespians, and musicians who thrive on artistic expression. A musical program may not excite students as much as seeing a favorite performing artist in concert, but your cultural arts programs can combine artistry and pragmatism. In high schools everywhere, students of all musical tastes are forming bands and singing at weddings, quinceañeras, and dances. Many of these ambitious students are struggling to find their niche as recording artists. Programs that give aspiring musicians (or actors, or writers) practical information about their dream profession can have astounding results. Allow cultural arts organizations to support your efforts.

Dance and drill team classes rarely find time or motivation to use the library media center. Imagine the impact of a program starring a member of a local dance troupe. If you live near a large city with a symphony, opera company, or ballet troupe, contact those organizations. Many will send representative artists to schools to perform. For example, one drill team instructor in Dallas joined with her library media specialist to host a program in the girls' gym. A local ballerina gave a talk titled, "What to Do Before the Music Starts," in which she taught special breathing techniques and stretching exercises. When the library media specialist learned the specific content of the presentation, she invited the district's trainer/physical therapist to share information about preventing injuries or tending to them if they occur. During the planning stages, the media specialist noticed a packet of coupons in the teacher's lounge offering faculty a free month's membership at a local gym. She called the sales representative to find such a deal for students. Although she couldn't get students month-long trial memberships, she did secure three guest passes for every program participant. By program time, the media specialist had created a network consisting of a community business, a fine arts elective, the health/athletic department, and a cultural arts organization.

Nearly all professions have their own organizations where members grow professionally and personally through meetings, workshops, and social events. Look into organizations related to businesses of particular interest to your local community. Easier still, notice what opportunities exist in your own profession. One visit to the exhibits at state or national library conventions illustrates just how many companies travel to schools to promote reading, teach research skills, or offer on-campus computer training. In just one exhibit hall you have numerous program ideas and opportunities laid out before you.

Be creative in considering the abundant possibilities for program help. Both honorary and social sororities and fraternities may provide tremendous program contributions. Conservation groups may want to share programs related to ecology. Psychiatric organizations may have resources related to mental health (teens dealing with depression) or physical ailments (eating disorders). Check the newspapers. Trials bring out organizations for and against major issues. Hot topics such as teen smoking, drivers using cellular telephones, and Internet scams attract organizations that might have valuable information to share with health classes, driver's education students, or computer clubs, respectively. For hotly debated topics, your program can give students balanced information to make informed decisions.

All types of organizations can support programming. Whether they send materials, provide guest experts, or simply connect you with online resources, organizations are worth contacting. Figure 4.5 lists organizations that frequently support programs for high schools, along with sample program titles.

Clubs and Organizations	Program Titles
Aquatic club	Dolphin Therapy for Special Needs Children
Bankers' association	College Without Poverty
Historical society	Footprints of History in Your own Backyard
Humane society	For the Life of Your Pet
Junior Achievement	Small Businesses, Big Ideas
Musician's organization	Tejano in the Mainstream
Sierra Club	Earth Day Every Day: 101 Ways to Save the Planet
Writer's group	Teen-friendly Publishers for Fiction and Poetry

Figure 4.5. Examples of organizations and clubs, with program titles.

In addition to the organizations in Figure 4.5, consider the following:

Book clubs	Cultural arts organizations (theater, symphony, ballet, opera)
Cultural groups (heritage societies, ethnic groups)	Fraternities and sororities
Hobby-related groups	Medical-related charities and foundations
Pet clubs	Political organizations
Professional organizations	Retired professionals' organizations
Area sports organizations	Major sports organizations (NFL, WNBA)
Sports clubs (tennis, ski, swim)	Various special interest organizations and clubs

Government Agencies

National, state, and local government agencies have a wealth of materials and resource people available for schools. Agencies not only can provide program speakers, but they also can supply information (brochures, pamphlets) for your vertical file and reference section. Foreign government agencies also share resources through their consulates and embassies. (Figure 4.6 lists some government agencies that support secondary curriculum, with sample program titles.) Addresses and telephone numbers for the government agencies are available in the telephone directory, online telephone listings, and at their individual Web sites. Chapter 6 lists Web site addresses for government agencies, along with detailed information each offers.

U.S. Government Agencies	Program Titles
National Aeronautics and Space Administration	Aboard the Space Shuttle
Federal Aviation Agency	Highways in the Sky
U.S. Postal Service	Online Services
U.S. Department of Immigration & Naturalization	Becoming a Citizen
Federal Bureau of Investigation	Invisible Clues: DNA
National Parks Service	Practical Conservation
Department of Public Safety	Defensive Driving
Fire Department	Volunteers and Careers
Police Department	Scared Straight: One Day Inside a Corrections Facility
Municipal Court	A View from a Judge's Bench
Mayor's Office (or City Manager)	What It Takes to Run Your City
Parks and Recreation Department	What's There for You?

Figure 4.6. Examples of government agencies, with sample program titles.

In addition to those listed in Figure 4.6, explore the following government agencies:

Department of Agriculture   Drug Enforcement Administration
Foreign consulates and embassies   Local government agencies
Branches of the armed services   National Marine Fisheries Service
National Weather Service   United States Congress
United States Customs Service   United States Mint
United States Supreme Court

Media

Newspapers, television stations, radio stations, and magazines can connect you to resources. Pay special attention to local newspapers and Sunday supplements, especially sections on "upcoming events," "happenings," or "what's going on in the community." These resources announce presentations by authors, scientists, actors, and sports stars. Movies and live dramatic productions of classics provide potential programming ideas. Often, theaters will announce performances held expressly for students at no cost or for nominal fees. Let teachers schedule the field trip while you prepare a related program before or after they see the production.

Holidays and Special Events

Although programs with holiday or special event themes are more common in elementary schools, they make outstanding programs for high school students, too. In addition to standard choices such as Halloween, Easter, and Valentine's Day, cover holidays honoring special people, such as Columbus Day or Martin Luther King Jr. Day.

Keep abreast of local holidays, like the Strawberry Festival in Pasadena, Texas, or Founders Days in many regions, to capitalize on great ideas, resources, and collaborations. Community events also generate program ideas. Fishing tournaments, hot air balloon festivals, and the Walk of Historic Homes are all local celebrations that you can support through programming. Besides checking your community's calendar of events, contact event organizers to request materials and guest speakers. Rather than developing an independent event, volunteer to host one portion of a large program created and funded by the community.

When generating program ideas for national holidays, incorporate a reading component for added relevance. Offer holiday programs associated with literary classics, such as O Henry's "The Gift of the Magi" at Christmas, Truman Capote's "The Thanksgiving Visitor," and Walt Whitman's "When Lilacs Last in the Dooryard Bloom'd" for President's Day. If you don't have these resources in your media center, borrow them through interlibrary loan. Check Web sites about these authors for biographical information and support materials.

Sometimes holiday programs come from unexpected sources. An unsuccessful English lesson in Georgia turned into a program centering around Italy's carnival season and Edgar Allan Poe's "The Cask of Amantillado." When her students found the story's language too rich for independent reading, the teacher collaborated with the library media specialist on a program that enriched their vocabulary and taught them about the carnival celebration. The teacher devised an interactive vocabulary game, and the media specialist prepared a presentation with facts gathered from a travel agent and decorations from a party store. In one program, students received a vocabulary and cultural lesson.

Chambers of Commerce

Chambers of Commerce have abundant information about local events. Each year, members compile a community calendar listing holidays, meetings, celebrations, festivals, and other happenings. They are among the most informed and diverse resource connections you will find, and they can help at every stage of programming. Trying to decide on a relevant program topic? Consider offering a program that coincides with a community event listed on the calendar. Need help contacting local professionals? Your local chamber can provide names, telephone numbers, and contact persons for nearby businesses as well as organizations and clubs. Having trouble finding a talented guest speaker? The chamber can also connect you to speakers' bureaus with experts on many special topics. Develop a positive rapport with your Chamber of Commerce. It is likely to be among your best program resources.

Conclusion

Almost any educational resource, whether purchased, rented, or made, can support programming. Identifying the most appropriate resources for your topic and audience gives your search clarity. Knowing where to find these resources in your school, district, and community gives it direction. Armed with this information, you can quickly select effective and economical program resources.

Chapter 5

How to Gather and Organize Resources

When doing research, navigating the online catalog and finding possible resources only begins the process. You must also know how to use available materials. Similarly, knowing where to find program resources is only a first step. Next, you must learn how to select the best resources. For example, choosing an outstanding speaker for a program demands far different skills than finding an appropriate video clip or ordering an exhibit from a museum. Different resources require different approaches.

Selecting Volunteers

When selecting volunteer resources, consider the people most easily accessible to the school: parents, students, and teachers. All can be helpful volunteers with knowledge related to curriculum or student interests. To choose volunteers most suited to your program needs, gather data through surveys or questionnaires.

Parents

Many parents are eager to help at their child's school but cannot make long-term volunteer commitments. However, they might be available to speak or help at a single school library media program. As speakers, they can share professional experiences, leisure activities, travel adventures, or expertise on their favorite topics. Some may give fine demonstrations or make impressive media presentations. Even parents unable to share their time can contribute to a program by providing materials for displays or exhibits.

You can easily gather information on parents' interests and expertise by sending them surveys at the beginning of the year. First, meet with your principal to request permission to distribute the surveys. To make the most of this meeting,

- Begin by summarizing your plans for school library media programs;
- Describe the need for program resources;
- Explain the reasons for sending the survey;
- Discuss the benefits (to students, faculty, and you) of using parents as resources; and
- Share with your principal a copy of the survey and letter that you will send to parents.

After securing the principal's permission, stress to teachers the far-reaching value of your survey. Explain that you will organize and file the surveys, then make them available for their use. Then ask them to help get the surveys out to parents through the children. (Figure 5.1 is an example of a survey that can be sent to parents.)

Survey results identify parents' specific knowledge, skills, unique possessions, non-print materials, and hobbies. They also indicate in what capacity each parent is able to volunteer. Regardless of the survey format, request several ways to contact parents. Beyond this requirement, mold the survey to fit the programming needs of your particular facility.

Students

Sometimes the surveys you send to parents may mention a son's or daughter's collections and special hobbies. More often, you will discover students' interests just by interacting with them. Although students may not have much public speaking experience, their enthusiasm and knowledge can captivate an audience of their peers. With a little coaching on how to streamline their presentations, students may become primary contributors to your most riveting programs.

Teachers

After gathering survey data, enter all relevant information into a community resources file. (Details for establishing the community resources file appear in the next section.) Then make the file available to teachers. Also, foster a positive rapport with your colleagues by repaying them for helping to distribute the surveys. As you learn about teachers' lessons, special projects, and classroom programs, flip through your files to find possible volunteers. A brief note or tip about potential parent support can be invaluable to teachers. Even if you don't have specific recommendations, occasionally remind colleagues that your files are available for their perusal.

Dear Parents:

Our school library media center is gathering ideas for special programs to offer as a means of supporting and enriching curriculum. If you have a hobby, special talent, skill, interest, or travel experience that you would like to share, please complete the survey below and return it to your child's teacher.

Thank you,
Rico Esparza
Library Media Specialist

Date _____

COMMUNITY RESOURCES QUESTIONNAIRE

_____ Yes, I would like to share information/materials with the students at Loretta Tonge High School.

Name _____ Phone _____

Name(s) of Children   Name(s) of Teacher(s)

_____   _____

_____   _____

Special Hobbies/Crafts:
    Description of hobby/craft: _____

_____

    _____ I would be willing to discuss it with students.
    _____ I would be willing to demonstrate it.
    _____ I would be willing to share it with students as an exhibit.

Special Talents/Skills:
    Description of talent/skill: _____

_____

    _____ I would be willing to discuss it with students.
    _____ I would be willing to demonstrate it.
    _____ I would be willing to contribute materials for a display.
    _____ I would be willing to share my storytelling ability with students.

Travel Experiences:
    Description (places): _____
    _____ I would like to discuss it with students.
    _____ I have slides, films, or photographs to share with students.
    _____ I have interesting materials from this country to contribute to
        a display.

Figure 5.1. Community resources questionnaire for parents.

Photo 5.1. At Duchesne Academy in Houston, Texas, media specialist Barbara Weathers answers questions from student volunteers Angelica Sandrea and Michelle Mitchell.

Finally, consider teachers as another program resource. Many departments are filled with outstanding teaching materials that enhance programming. Even though teachers are already overworked, some are rejuvenated by sharing a special skill and interest not related to their curriculum. To discover their interests, give teachers a survey similar to that in Figure 5.1. Encourage them to record hobbies, collections, travel experiences, and skills they might present to students.

The teachers' survey offers three other benefits: It makes teachers more aware of what the school library media center has to offer their students, it encourages them to look for possible resources to add to the file, and it adds teacher recommendations to your list of program resources.

Making It Work With Volunteers

Recruiting and working with volunteers is essential for programming. Usually, parents help plan, prepare, and present programs. At other times, they fulfill regular media center duties while you and other volunteers work on special programs. Some prefer to share their skills and talents by volunteering as guest speakers. In any role, they are a valuable resource whose support should not be underestimated.

Parent volunteers can also help you develop a community resources file. After generating a set of questions for potential community resources, ask parent volunteers to make the telephone contacts. After these volunteers record their information, another volunteer can be in charge of developing and updating the resources file.

Prepare for Volunteers

To gather a parent volunteer team, know the district policy on obtaining volunteers. In some districts, policies are open-ended, leaving decisions to campus administrators. Others specify exact requirements for who may have volunteers, how many they may recruit, how they can be acquired, and how they should be assessed throughout the year. Almost all districts have set rules about bringing volunteers into their buildings. In this era of heightened security concerns, follow the district or campus guidelines to the letter. In those rare cases where a written policy is not already in place, suggest creating one with the campus site-based committee or the faculty at large.

No matter what the circumstance, secure the principal's permission for whatever you do. It may take a dash of diplomacy and more than one meeting to convince the principal that you even need volunteers. Be persuasive and persistent. Even if you have support staff, volunteers are integral to program success.

After receiving permission to recruit or add more volunteers, keep the principal abreast of every stage of your volunteer program. Share a copy of the Volunteer Form (see Figure 5.2). Update the principal on successes you owe to volunteer support. Most important, introduce parent volunteers to the principal (and his or her secretary) when they first begin working, then invite the principal to the library media center occasionally to see how much the volunteers are contributing to the school.

Recruit Volunteers

Simple forms are often the most successful recruiting tools. Succinct, direct requests set a professional tone. Parents who volunteer regularly will respect your efficiency. Although they are working for free, they want their volunteer time to be productive. Parents who have never volunteered or worked in a modern school library media center may be apprehensive. Well-written request forms make good impressions. If they alone don't inspire cooperation, the information they provide may lead to future interactions that will. Figure 5.2 is a sample request for parent volunteer help, and Figure 5.3 is a sample form asking volunteers what tasks they would like to do.

Contacting Resources

Although you will set your own program goals and make all final decisions about program content, you can delegate many other responsibilities to volunteers. Contacting resource people and organizing the contact information may not be difficult tasks, but they are important. Good programs need good contact people and material resources. Finding them and accessing information about them require communication and organizational skills.

Dear Parents:

Our school library media center needs your help. To keep the media center functioning at maximum potential, we depend on parent volunteers who make it possible to carry out unique activities and programs. Would you be willing to work in the school library media center several hours per week? If not, could you help us by performing some duties at home? Please complete the following questionnaire if you are interested in volunteering in any capacity. Your consideration is greatly appreciated.

Library Media Center Volunteer Form

Name: _____   Days and times available to work in LMC:

Address: _____   _____

Phone: _____   _____

E-mail: _____   _____

Name(s) of Child(ren):   Name(s) of Homeroom Teacher(s)

_____   _____

_____   _____

_____   _____

Special Skills/Talents/Interests:

_____ Word processing   _____ Artwork/graphics

_____ Internet research   _____ Laminating

_____ Read aloud   _____ Filing

_____ Storytelling   _____ Book repair

Other type of work: _____

Figure 5.2. Volunteer recruitment form for parents.

List Possible Resources

Prepare your volunteers for contacting possible resources. Begin by describing your program goals and the resources you think can support them. Then discuss with your volunteers the campus, district, and community resources listed in Chapter 4. Help your volunteers begin their searches. Guide them to references that initiate their searches. District contact lists, local telephone directories, and Internet search engines may all be fine starting points for locating resources. Be available to answer questions or offer help, but trust that your volunteers can handle the task alone. This process is not difficult. It just takes time and a little tenacity.

Volunteer Task Request

Volunteer's Name: _____

Phone number: _____

Days and Times Available: _____

Please check the library media center tasks that interest you:

_____ Word Processing
_____ Working at circulation desk
_____ Laminating
_____ Helping to process books
_____ Helping to develop learning centers
_____ Contacting resources and recording information in resource file
_____ Repairing damaged books
_____ Shelving books
_____ Processing audiovisual materials
_____ Maintaining vertical file
_____ Supervising reference area
_____ Assisting with displays and exhibits
_____ Filing cards

Figure 5.3. Volunteer task request form (to be given to volunteers after orientation).

Interview Potential Resources

After your volunteers have a list of contacts, let them conduct telephone interviews to determine what program support each contact can provide. Suggest that volunteers keep the interview succinct. They should begin by introducing themselves, then explain that they have called to secure program support. Immediately after, volunteers should ask predetermined questions like those listed below. Whenever possible, tailor questions to the goals of a particular program.

1. Do you know a teacher or parent at this school?

2. Are you interested in sharing information about your field of expertise, skills, or area of interest with high school students?

3. Are you willing to visit (or send people from your business) to our school?

4. What would you (or your business) like to offer students?

5. Do you think you can tailor the information to high school students?

6. Do you have program material already prepared?

7. What is the length of time needed for the program?

8. What types of information will you share during the presentation?

9. Will you need computer or audiovisual equipment?

10.   Are there certain days that you are available?

11.   How much notice do you require to share a prepared presentation?

12.   How much notice do you require to develop a presentation for one of our programs?

13.   Do you charge a speaking fee?

14.   Could you supply any handouts to the students?

15.   Would you be able to provide materials for a display or exhibit?

During the interview, volunteers should record information in an organized manner. After asking the predetermined questions, they can request brochures or pamphlets that provide more information. Finally, volunteers should thank the contact person but leave the final statement open-ended. They may say, "Thank you for your time. I will share this information with the media specialist." Or, "Thank you for sharing this information. You've been very helpful." Be sure volunteers do not state or imply that someone will call back. Even if the contact seems promising, you may find a better, more convenient, or less-expensive resource. Or you may end up changing your program plans. Leave your options open, and do not let volunteers create expectations that you may not fulfill.

After the telephone interviews, review the information and, if necessary, discuss that contact person further with your volunteers. Primarily, decide if the information on this contact is worth recording for future use. Based on curricular needs and student interests, is this person or business a good potential resource for future programs? If the answer is yes, then record the information on the community resources card. Over time, the resources cards, brochures, and pamphlets should be organized for easy access.

Organizing the Resources

After identifying and contacting resources from the community, organize the resources. Use whatever method makes most sense to you. Volunteers are temporary. In subsequent years, you are the one who will need to find those contact lists, resources, and materials. Create whatever system will enable you to access information quickly and explain the system easily to teachers and future volunteers. Both a community resources file and a vertical file can help.

Establish a Community Resources File

Creating a community resources file for the campus or district is worthwhile for all types of program development, including special programs initiated by teachers and administrators. Place resource data into a separate card file organized in whatever way seems most appropriate. Some media specialists like a straightforward alphabetized arrangement of all resources. Others organize them by the different types of resources identified in Chapter 4. Still others file resources according to the programs for which they were used.

Instead of keeping a separate resources file, you may prefer to store resource data with other program materials. For easy access, you may store background information, notes on modifications for next year, student art, and lists of resource people and materials in one file pocket. When you repeat the program, you'll find everything stored in one place.

Share Resources and Responsibilities

No matter what your preferred method of organization, inform department chairpersons or individual classroom teachers about the location and organization of program resources. Not only will this help them find materials when they plan a unit, but it also enables them to contribute more resources to the library media center when they find something new to add to the file.

Establishing a community resources file for a school seems like an overwhelming task, but it does not have to be. After making the commitment to develop such a file, lighten the load by assigning the work to parent volunteers. To start the process, implement the following steps:

Select Interested Parent Volunteers

When establishing the file, brainstorm with parent volunteers and teachers. Devise a systematic plan to develop the file. Then recruit a volunteer or two who enjoy projects involving organization and who can see the job through to completion. Usually when you discuss the project with volunteers, some will be genuinely interested. It is best if only one or two volunteers tackle the project; that way, they can better claim ownership of the work. The volunteers can pursue the project in the school library media center once a week. If they need more time, you may suggest they work on the project at home.

Determine the Best Format

Sometimes consistency makes finding resources easy. Consequently, some media specialists organize everything using the exact same format. Others look at the materials they must organize and determine the easiest way to store them now and access them again later. Whatever format you choose, keep it simple. Teachers should be able to search through the resources without your help. Following are the most common formats:

1. *Folder format.* Folders are arranged alphabetically by topic in a filing cabinet, much like a vertical file. In each folder, store flyers, pamphlets, handouts, photos, and information about the community resources. (See Figure 5.4 for a community resources sample form.)

2. *Small card format* (usually 3x5). Record all information on a single, small card, and include a notation about where to find related materials (see Figure 5.5).

3. *Large card format* (usually 4 x 6). Record information on the cards arranged in an appropriate-sized file box. Store the box near materials associated with the program.

4. *Electronic format.* If you have an online catalog system that uses standard MARC format, you may want to incorporate community resources information into the MARC format designed specifically for community resources. If you do not have an online catalog, you can develop your own community resources database using a database management program.

Community Resources Form

Topic _____ Date Entered _____

Name _____

Contact Person _____

Address _____

_____

Phone _____ Fax _____

E-Mail Address _____

Type of Program _____

Grade Levels _____

Length of Time Required _____

Equipment Needs _____

Availability _____

Fees _____

Program Description _____

_____

_____

_____

_____

Comments_____

_____

_____

Figure 5.4. Sample form for community resources file folder.

Topic _____ Date Entered _____

Name _____ Grade Levels _____

Address _____ Availability _____

_____ Equipment Needs: _____

Phone _____ _____

Fax _____ Fee _____

E-mail _____

Description _____

Comments _____

Figure. 5.5. Sample card for community resources file.

Determine What the File Should Contain

Regardless of the format you choose, record the following information on each card about every resource:

date

name of person, business, company, institution, club, agency

street and e-mail address

fax and phone number

time available

length of program

special audiovisual equipment needs

appropriate target group to which the resource will appeal (age, grade, etc.)

fees (if any)

general program description

Also include a brief evaluation of the resource after using it and the date of the evaluation. For example, after a program with a guest speaker, record personal observations and feedback from teachers and students about the speaker on the reverse side of the form or card.

Determine File Arrangement

Arranging the file is important, especially if it will be used by faculty, staff, and administrators. Consider the following arrangements:

- Arrange alphabetically by name of person or business.
- Arrange alphabetically by topic to which that resource contributes.
- Arrange by subject area.
- Cross reference by name, topic, and subject area.

Determine Who May Use the File

It is best to make the community resources file available to all faculty at your school, administrators, other media specialists in the district, and in some cases, students working on projects. When school library media specialists and the local public library staff work together and share files, patrons of both benefit, and the work of maintaining a file is easier to justify. By sharing, everyone has access to more resources.

Because so few media specialists have a community resources file, some industrious media specialists join together to establish one file to be shared among campuses. Thanks to the common practice of interlibrary loan, even students are familiar with the concept of shared resources.

Publicize the Availability of the File

For the file to be used, you must advertise its availability to teachers, the principal, parents, students, and others in the district. Share your rationale for developing the file and remind everyone that its existence enhances programs in the classroom and throughout the school. Not only will the file help you develop programs, but it also encourages teachers to begin programming. Even if they never use the file for anything else, teachers will be grateful to you for providing access to guest speakers.

Revise the File Regularly

Determine a policy for updating the file and add it to the formal school library media center policy manual. Updates of the community resource file are necessary. As most library media specialists know, this task is much like the weeding process. Although the work is not difficult, finding time to do it may be a challenge. Therefore, assign the job of keeping up with the community resources file to one or two volunteers who enjoy this type of work. Let them be responsible for deleting inaccurate or outdated contact information as well as adding new or updated data. Simply verifying the information every year or two will ensure easy contact when you need it.

Conclusion

Library media specialists who know how to find, gather, and organize resources are well equipped to put together truly dynamic programs. Knowledge of the resources both within and beyond the community can support programming in the most vital way. It transforms ordinary, predictable programs into riveting events rich in content and extended learning.

Chapter 6

Searching the Internet
for Resources

The Internet's expansiveness and rapid growth afford previously unimaginable access to information. However, this benefit gives rise to two concerns: Web sites can come and go very quickly, and all Web sites require the discerning eye of educators to ensure that the information given is accurate. Taking these two concerns into consideration, we have compiled a list of outstanding Web sites that will support library programming. All sites were accessed in September 2001.

This chapter includes Web sites for three different categories that will support and enrich library programs:

1. Resources to Support Curriculum

    Business and Industry

    Government Agencies

    Institutions

    Virtual Field Trips

    Young Adult Literature

2. Resources to Support Teen Interests

    Colleges and Careers

    General Interest

    Newspapers and Periodicals Online

    Sports

3. Resources to Support Media Specialists and Teachers

    Copyright

Curriculum

General Resources

Professional Associations

Professional Journals Online

The Web sites listed in the first group correspond to the community resources discussed in Chapter 4. Other Web sites provided in this chapter relate to high school curriculum, teen interests, and resources for media specialists and teachers. Sites for popular young adult authors are also included in the first section.

Some of these Web sites were created expressly for educators. Others include pages specifically designed for teens. Every Web site contains valuable information for media specialists, teachers, and high school students.

Sites indicated with an asterisk (*) offer excellent starting points because they provide links to numerous other resources related to the specific category. All sites listed support programming in the following ways:

- You may gather ideas to plan and develop programs.
- You may gain more information on the program topic.
- You may locate resources, including people, exhibits, activities, pamphlets, and other supplemental resources.
- Teachers may acquire information and activities to prepare students for upcoming programs.
- Students may access the Web sites to research a program topic, participate in online activities, or take virtual field trips to extend and reinforce learning.

Resources to Support the Curriculum

Many of the Web sites listed here were created expressly for students and teachers to use as educational tools. All of the areas, particularly the author section, have obvious connections to school library media center programming. Web sites with a more general interest base can meaningfully serve the same purpose. Businesses and government agencies support math, science, and social studies. Institutions enhance programs in those core curriculum areas, as well as electives. They prove especially relevant for fine arts classes, because museums in particular develop many educational resources (often for free) to support educational programs. As you explore these possibilities, note that we chose these Web sites because their strong content offers direct support to curriculum.

Business and Industry

Knowing where to find listings of businesses within your community and across the United States can speed up your planning stage considerably. In addition to providing extensive information, businesses and corporations are excellent resources for finding guest speakers, supplemental material, and even financial support for programming.

SuperPages

http://www.superpages.com

This site lists businesses by category or state and has educational links to reference sources and resources for teachers.

* *Guide to the Web*

http://www.theactgroup.com/webguide_directories.htm

This extensive site contains the following sections, which provide access to various resources:

"Switchboard"—nationwide telephone and address directory

"InfoSpace"—personal, business, and government phone, fax, and e-mail numbers/addresses

"Anywho"—AT&T's clear directory also includes a reverse directory

"Zip2 Yellow Pages"—search businesses by name, category, or distance from home

"Directory of toll free numbers from Infospace"—quick access to toll free numbers

"Big Yellow"—national business yellow pages and residential listings from NYNEX

"Thomas Register of Manufacturers"—the most complete list of manufacturers

"WhoWhere"—an e-mail address database

"Zip Code and Zip + 4 Finder"—a simple and efficient zip code directory

* *Smartpages.com*

http://http1.smartpages.com/

This online directory of business listings and city and shopping guides is designed to help consumers shop; research products and services; locate merchants; and plan entertainment, leisure, and travel activities.

Government Agencies

Many government agencies have Web sites that can enrich library programs. Some sites include pages specifically designed for educators. Access these sites to research a program topic, develop program ideas, gather resources, and plan activities.

Gradually, these sites have added components directed to students. As a result, you might also encourage students to visit some sites before or after attending your program to further explore the topic. While there, they can learn about the topic and participate in entertaining activities. Also, note that many government sites include areas for teachers and parents. Some contain virtual tours and online libraries that offer maps, photographs, and other helpful resources.

Air Force

http://www.af.mil/

This online gallery offers photographs and detailed information about topics such as U.S. Air Force operations, careers, and aircraft. Portraits and information about current and past leaders is also available. Teens especially like the section that highlights active and retired aircraft. (The other branches of the military also have their own sites.)

CIA

http://www.odci.gov/cia/ciakids/

This interactive and fun-filled site explains the functions and background of the CIA. It also offers a virtual tour of the CIA. Students will particularly enjoy the "CIA Canine Corp.," "Try a Disguise," and the "CIA Exhibit Center."

*Department of Health and Human Services

http://www.hhs.gov/

This site provides useful links to numerous other sites that contain information about different federal agencies. All of these sites, some of which are listed individually in this chapter, focus on teaching teens about the agencies through activities and games.

FBI for Kids and Youth

http://www.fbi.gov/kids/kids.htm

Students can learn a great deal about the FBI at this site, which is divided into three visitor levels: kids (K–5), youth (6–12), and parent/teacher. A special Department of Justice (DOJ) page teaches about forensics, DNA and polygraph testing, and fingerprinting. In the areas such as "Working Dogs," "Crime Detection," and "Crime Prevention," students learn about the different departments of the FBI. The "Most Wanted" and "Major Investigations" sections are popular with teens. A huge library arranged by topic offers a multitude of information about crime. This interesting site also provides career information.

Federal Emergency Management Agency (FEMA)

http://www.fema.gov/

Here, students can learn about different types of natural disasters, including tornadoes, earthquakes, and hurricanes. In addition to general weather information, this site teaches safety tips, including a section that helps families prepare for disasters.

*Louisiana State University, "A List of Federal Agencies on the Internet"

http://www.lib.lsu.edu/gov/exec.html

Maintained by Louisiana State University, this site lists all the U.S. federal government agencies on the Internet and links them to their sites. It has two main divisions: "Executive Branch and Agencies" and "Independent Establishments and Government Corporations." Subheadings for each are the same and include "Judicial"; "Legislative"; "Independent"; "Boards, Commissions, and Committees"; "Quasi-Official"; and "Complete U.S. Federal Government Agencies Directory."

National Aeronautics and Space Administration (NASA) Education Program

http://education.nasa.gov/

Linked to A Guide to NASA's Education Programs, this searchable database contains brief descriptions of NASA's education programs, including points of contact, admission criteria, location, content areas, and financial support for all of NASA's field centers. Visitors can access a variety of educational programs, materials, and services. Here you will find contact information and resources arranged by NASA field centers, states, and regions throughout the United States.

National Archives and Records Administration, "The Digital Classroom"

http://www.nara.gov/education/classrm.html

To encourage teachers at all levels to use archival documents in the classroom, "The Digital Classroom" shares materials from the National Archives and methods for teaching with primary sources.

*National Park Service

http://www.nps.gov/

This central hub for almost all of the 375 sites found in the National Park System connects educators to numerous sites focusing on "America's natural and cultural heritage through the National Parks." Web pages range from publications, video presentations, and guided walks and talks to extensive curriculum-based education programs.

U.S. Department of Energy

http://www.science.doe.gov/

Students and educators can visit this site to learn more about science, technology, energy, engineering, and math. Interesting activities enrich the learning experience.

U.S. Department of Treasury

http://www.ustreas.gov/education.html

Students can find information on topics such as U.S. coins, paper money, and our national bank system. The "Treasury's Learning Vault" focuses on topics such as the history of our Treasury and provides a library packed with related resources. A favorite area is the "U.S Mint," which shares basic information about how money is minted.

White House

http://www.whitehouse.gov/

Take an online tour of the White House and meet the president and first lady. Learn about White House history and tour its gallery of art. "Gateway to Government" provides links to the president's cabinet. Viewers are encouraged to send mail to the president, vice president, and their spouses.

Institutions

Because many are directly linked to education, institutions are among the best resources to support programming. Rather than sharing only general information, many of these Web sites offer activities for students, interactive games, teacher resources, and online libraries. Many also guide visitors through virtual tours of exhibits and galleries. When planning your program, take advantage of the extensive information most of these sites share on a variety of topics. (Many can provide guest speakers, exhibits, and materials to support science, math, social studies, and the arts.)

Aquariums

National Aquarium in Baltimore
http://www.aqua.org/

This Web site invites guests to dive in to discover information about animals, exhibits, conservation efforts, and the institution itself. "Aquarium Fact Sheets," "College Internship Opportunities," and a teachers' section will be of interest to students and educators.

UnderWater World
http://www.underwaterworld.com/

Visit UnderWater World at the Mall of America in Bloomington, Minnesota, and you can take a trip not only through, but also under, the aquarium's exhibits: a Minnesota lake, the Mississippi River, the Gulf of Mexico, and a Caribbean reef.

University of Hawaii, "The Waikiki Aquarium"
http://www.mic.hawaii.edu/aquarium/

This outstanding site offers a beautiful virtual tour where users can click on any creature to gain information about it. The library area provides a searchable database of Web sites and resources about the aquarium, its exhibits, and Hawaiian and South Pacific marine life.

Colleges, Universities, and Schools

**All About College*
http://www.allaboutcollege.com/

At *All About College* you'll find thousands of links to colleges and universities around the world, including admissions office e-mail addresses for most schools. The list includes colleges in the United States, Canada, Mexico, Africa, Asia, Europe, Australia, and South America.

**American School Directory*
http://www.asd.com/

Want to see what's going on at other schools across the nation? Here you can access more than 70,000 school sites. By visiting the individual school sites, library media specialists can acquire a wealth of exciting ideas related to special events, curriculum, and activities.

**American Universities and Colleges*
http://www.globalcomputing.com/universy.html

This site provides a complete listing of universities and colleges that can be accessed by the name of the college or the state.

Libraries

Herbert Hoover Presidential Library and Museum
http://www.hoover.nara.gov/

When using the Internet for program enrichment, don't forget about the wealth of information that can be found at presidential libraries. This site focuses on Herbert Hoover's life and accomplishments.

Library of Congress
http://lcweb.loc.gov/

Browse this huge site to become familiar with abundant information available to support media center programs. The online gallery shares overviews of Library of Congress exhibitions. The "Fun Site for Kids and Family" offers a variety of learning experiences for youngsters and teens. For example, "Meet Amazing Americans" presents photographs and detailed information about famous inventors, politicians, performers, and activists.

New York Public Library
http://www.nypl.org

This site has everything imaginable for library users: catalogs, a digital library collection, archival collections, health information, and electronic resources. "Teen Link" provides recommended booklists and links teens to categories such as fun, sports, and homework help. "TV & Movies" is a popular spot for teens.

Museums

*Smithsonian Institution
http://www.si.edu/info/museums_research.htm

This address takes you to the general information site of the Smithsonian Institution, with links to its various museums and galleries, zoos, and research facilities. Each of these areas has its own Web site, with opportunities for excellent online tours, activities, and teacher information. The site also offers a useful alphabetical listing of subject areas to help organize the vast information available.

Air and Space

The International Women's Air and Space Museum
http://www.iwasm.org/

Like the museum now located at Burke Lakefront Airport in Dayton, Ohio, this site is dedicated to "preserving the history of women in aviation." Biographical information, photographs, and interesting facts about women who have made major contributions to aviation and space are available.

National Air and Space Museum
http://www.nasm.si.edu/nasm/edu/

This site contains information and activities about aviation and space topics such as the exploration of the universe. Be sure to investigate the educational links, the online galleries, and the special area for teachers.

Art

* Yahooligans: Arts and Entertainment: Art: Museums and Galleries
http://www.yahooligans.com/Arts_and_Entertainment/Art/Museums_and_Galleries/

This excellent site links visitors to more than 75 different museums and galleries, including the Smithsonian, the Guggenheim Museum, and the Library of Congress: American Treasures. The listing is alphabetical and includes a brief description of the museum or gallery. Some of the outstanding art museum sites that can be accessed follow:

Fine Arts Museum of San Francisco, http://www.thinker.org/

Louvre Museum, http://www.louvre.fr/louvrea.htm

The Metropolitan Museum of Art, http://www.metmuseum.org/

National Gallery of Art, http://www.nga.gov/

Smithsonian Institution: National Museum of American Art, http://www.nmaa.si.edu/

Visitors to these sites will discover virtual tours of galleries, in-depth looks at specific artists and works of art, and virtual tours of current or past exhibits. Many of these sites list services for teachers and schools, teaching resources, and information to use when visiting the galleries.

History

National Museum of the American Indian
http://www.si.edu/nmai/

The museum, located in Washington, D.C., highlights the history of the American Indian. The Web site provides detailed information about the various programs offered.

Smithsonian Institution, "National Museum of American History"
http://americanhistory.si.edu/youmus/rscteach.htm

This site's well-designed virtual exhibitions cover a variety of topics, such as "The American Presidency" and "Star Spangled Banner." This site offers a plethora of information to enrich American history projects.

Science

American Museum of Natural History
http://www.amnh.org/

One of the world's finest museums, located in New York City, can be accessed online. You don't want to miss the virtual tours (complete with sound) of the museum's various exhibits. Be sure to browse the online version of the museum's popular journal, *Natural History*.

Franklin Institute
http://sln.fi.edu/

Take an online journey and learn about science topics and exhibits at this Philadelphia museum. Science educators and media specialists planning a science-related program will find links to Internet resources, games, puzzles, science activities, and lessons.

Museum of Science: Boston
http://www.mos.org/

Viewers of this site can visit excellent online exhibits. For example, "The Virtual Fish Tank" turns your computer into an aquarium. Various activities, resources, and Web links make this an excellent resource for enriching science programs.

The Museum of Science, Art and Human Perception, "The Exploratorium"
http://www.exploratorium.edu/

Housed in San Francisco's Palace of Fine Arts, the Exploratorium is a "collage of 650 science, art, and human perception exhibits." These exhibits are highlighted at this site, and a digital library of 10,000 pages of the *Exploratorium* Web site provides information on a vast array of topics.

Smithsonian Institution, "National Museum of Natural History"
http://www.mnh.si.edu/

This is another fine individual site developed by the Smithsonian Institution. The numerous topics highlighted at this site are packed with interesting information and photographs. Electronic field trips, educational resources, and exhibits make this site a top resource when developing library programs.

Zoos

Bronx Zoo
http://www.bronxzoo.com/

The Bronx Zoo in New York is home to more than 4,000 animals, including some of the world's most endangered species. Be sure to take an online tour of the zoo. For example, students won't want to miss the "Congo Virtual Tour," where they can meet Congo residents and play a Congo game.

* Conservation Breeding Specialist Group: Global Zoo Directory
http://www.cbsg.org/gzd.htm

This comprehensive directory of zoos around the world provides links to various sites and information on the nature of each institution's collection.

London Zoo
http://www.zsl.org/londonzoo/

Established in 1828 and open to the public since 1847, the London Zoo has long been one of the most famous zoos in the world. Visit this site and take a guided tour through the zoo, gather activities, and learn the latest news about the animal residents.

San Diego Zoo
http://www.sandiegozoo.org/

This interactive and information-packed site is a must. Learn facts about animals and zoos as you visit such spots as the "Virtual Photo Album." Photographs, videos, and interactive activities make this an excellent site for enriching library programs.

Smithsonian Institution, "National Zoo"
http://www.si.edu/natzoo/

At this Smithsonian Institution site, see the animals up close with the zoo's "Wild Webcams." On ZooTV you can see elephants, flamingoes, kiwis, and more. The animal video library allows an online view of the zoo's exhibits.

Virtual Field Trips

Although many sites previously listed include virtual field trips, a few more deserve mention. These Web sites prepare students for upcoming programs or reinforce learning afterward. Nearly every site includes special activities worth exploring.

GOALS—Global Online Adventure Learning Site, Inc.
http://www.goals.com/homebody.asp

GOALS provides educational adventures in science, technology, and nature. Adventures include a family voyage aboard a sailboat in the Pacific Ocean, a world tour using only human power, and a voyage to circumnavigate the world using oar power.

Passport to Knowledge
http://www.passporttoknowledge.com/

This outstanding site, supported by organizations such as the National Science Foundation, NASA, and public television, contains "interactive learning experiences using space-age telecommunications to connect students and teachers with our planet's leading researchers." The site encourages educators to move beyond the textbook and excite students about science by providing such activities as "Passport to Antarctica" and "Passport to the Rainforest." Online discussion groups, teacher support groups, and teacher resources are also provided.

Rice University's Virtual Tour, "Glacier"
http://www.glacier.rice.edu/

Rice University sponsors this virtual visit to Antarctica, developed by a graduate student, a polar explorer, and a high school teacher with the goals to create a Web site and develop "hands-on, inquiry based, thematic curriculum" for teachers and students. The site provides information and photographs of the region and its inhabitants.

The Virtual Field Trips Site
http://www.field-guides.com/

The virtual trips at this site are really tours through different Web sites to learn about subjects such as deserts, hurricanes, oceans, and volcanoes. Each field trip includes detailed lesson plans, with terms and concepts to learn before the trip, and other ideas, resources, and tools for the teacher and classroom.

*Yahoo! Recreation: Travel: Virtual Field Trips
http://dir.yahoo.com/recreation/travel/

This site provides more than 20 virtual field trips, including a bike journey in Africa, an archaeological excavation in Egypt, and Arctic adventures in Greenland.

Young Adult Literature

YA literature is more popular than ever. By tackling more diverse topics and targeting high school readers more directly, the authors are garnering credibility among and interest from teen readers as never before. No longer that vague genre between children's and adult literature, YA books and their authors have much to offer high school programs, as indicated by the following list of diverse Web sites.

Books and Awards

ALA Resources for Parents, Teens, and Kids
http://www.ala.org/parents

In the section designated expressly for them, teens can search specific pages such as "Book Lists from the Young Adult Library Service Association" and the "Michael L. Printz Award for Literary Excellence in Literature for Young Adults." For more extensive searches, they can explore the vast offerings from "Book Lists from the Young Adult Library Service Association" and the even more general "TEEN Hoopla: Internet Guide for Teens."

The ALAN Review
http://engfac.byu.edu/resources/alan/

In each issue, this journal from the National Council of the Teachers of English includes "Clip and File YA Book Reviews." Reviews of recently published young adult books include short summaries and bibliographic information.

Children's Book Awards
http://www.ucalgary.ca/~dkbrown/awards.html

This section of the Web site *The Children's Literature Web Guide* is "the most comprehensive guide to English-language children's book awards on the Internet." Although the site has not been updated for some time, it still offers links to many updated award sites. The "United States Awards" area lists all of the ALA awards as well as many others, including the Orbis Pictus Award for Outstanding Nonfiction for Children, The Scott O'Dell Award for Historical Fiction, and the Boston Globe-Horn Book Award.

Children's Literature Awards
http://www.norweld.lib.oh.us/ys/awards.htm

Sue McCleaf Nespeca of Youth Services, NORWELD, compiled this wonderful listing of "Web sites for various awards or prizes that are granted to children's literature titles." Each award listing includes a description of the award and a brief annotation about the Web site. All of the ALA awards are listed as well as the Boston Globe-Horn Book Awards, the *School Library Journal's* Best Books of the Year, Notable Social Studies Books for Young People, and many more.

Index to Internet Sites: Children's and Young Adult Authors & Illustrators
http://falcon.jmu.edu/~ramseyil/biochildhome.htm

This Internet School Library Media Center's section offers an index to author and illustrator sites. Besides the indexed sites, there are links to print bibliographies, author birthdays, interviews online, and author/illustrator appearances. The index is organized alphabetically and is very user friendly.

Kay Vandergrift's Young Adult Literature Page
http://www.scils.rutgers.edu/~kvander/YoungAdult/

Kay Vandergrift's site shares ideas and information about young adult literature. It begins with a discussion of a variety of issues about this type of literature. Then it offers links to bibliographies, other discussions, historical information, and related Web sites. The "Learning About the Author and Illustrator" pages offer a comprehensive listing of more than 600 links to authors and illustrators. A unique feature of the site is the listing of videos (including author videos) and CD-ROMs that support young adult literature.

Reading Rants!
http://tln.lib.mi.us/~amutch/jen/

This "out of the ordinary teen booklists" site lists books with a common theme such as "Gods and Monsters," "Inquiring Minds," "Boy Meets Book," and "Home Fries." Each list includes the title of the book and a short paragraph written for the young adult audience. Users can also search the site for specific titles.

Winning Titles (YALSA)
http://www.ala.org/yalsa/booklists/

YALSA created this site devoted to literature awards and lists specifically for young adults. The sections include "information on the award or list, a nomination form (when available), and links to current and previous winners or lists of titles." Some of the sections are "Outstanding Books for the College Bound," "Popular Paperbacks," "Quick Picks for Reluctant Young Adult Readers," "Selected Audio Books," and "Selected Videos and DVDs."

YA Literature
http://yahelp.suffolk.lib.ny.us/yalit.html

This section of the *Young Adult Librarian's Help/Homepage* offers a variety of links for teens. There is a "Booklists" area as well as "Popular YA Magazines" and "Comics and Graphic Novels." The site has links to other young adult literature areas, including Kay Vandergrift's excellent site and *Reading Rants!*

Young Adult Author Biographies

In this section we recommend a few of the many outstanding Web sites for the most popular young adult authors. Some of the addresses lead to publisher sites, others to the authors' personal Web sites. The Web sites for other young adult authors can be found easily by accessing the sites with an asterisk (*) listed at the beginning of this section or by visiting the site of the author's publishers. For example, the Kay Vandergrift site listed here offers a picture of the author, biography, bibliography, awards, address, and book reviews with summaries, then goes one step further, offering links to Web sites.

Biographical information about each author is usually available at the site. You will also find information about the author's works, including a complete bibliography. At most sites a photograph of the author, ways to contact the author, and frequently asked questions are provided. Some sites include links to interviews with the authors.

*Author Bios
http://www2.scholastic.com/teachers/authorsandbooks/authorsandbooks.jhtml

This Scholastic site includes biographies of a variety of authors, including YA favorites like Robert Cormier and S. E. Hinton. Each bio offers very personal information directly from the author with birthday, current city of residence, and a listing of awards. Users can then link to the author's booklist.

Index to Internet Sites: Children's and Young Adult Authors & Illustrators
http://falcon.jmu.edu/~ramseyil/biochildhome.htm

This Internet School Library Media Center's section offers an index to author and illustrator sites. In addition to the indexed sites, there are links to print bibliographies, author birthdays, interviews online, and author/illustrator appearances. The index is organized alphabetically and is very user friendly.

Kay Vandergrift's Young Adult Literature Page
http://www.scils.rutgers.edu/~kvander/YoungAdult/

The "Learning About the Author and Illustrator" pages offer a comprehensive listing of more than 600 links to authors and illustrators.

Mystery Writers
http://www.mysterywriters.net/

The Mystery Writers of America is the major organization for writers and other professionals in the mystery field. The site lists links to more than 75 MWA authors' sites, many of whose works high school students particularly enjoy.

Other popular YA author Web sites:

Bruce Brooks, http://www.scils.rutgers.edu/~kvander/brooks.html

Robert Cormier, http://www.randomhouse.com/teachers/authors/corm.html

Chris Crutcher, http://www.scils.rutgers.edu/~kvander/crutcher.html

Lois Duncan, http://www.iag.net/~barq/lois.html

S. E. Hinton, http://www.sehinton.com/

Lois Lowry, http://www.ipl.org/youth/AskAuthor/Lowry.html

Katherine Paterson, http://www.carolhurst.com/newsletters/31dnewsletters.html

Gary Paulsen, http://www.randomhouse.com/features/garypaulsen

Richard Peck, http://www.carolhurst.com/authors/rpeck.html

J. K. Rowling, http://www.scholastic.com/harrypotter/author/

Cynthia Voigt, http://www.scils.rutgers.edu/~kvander/voigt.html

Resources to Support Teen Interests

To increase patronage and book circulation, school library media specialists often create programs around teen interests. Understandably, programs on these themes are usually very successful in reshaping students' attitudes about the media center and about reading. When planning programs with a student interest theme, realize that the unlimited possibilities that exist prevent us from including all of them. Instead, we target major interests that could apply to a large cross-section of student populations, including sports, games, music, movies, and hobbies. Take special note of the "Colleges and Careers," "Sports," and "Newspapers and Periodicals" sites, because they provide multifaceted support for ideas, resources, and additional links.

Colleges and Careers

Photo 6.1. During the "Education and Career Center" program, students at Daviess High School in Owensboro, Kentucky, explore career options.

Whether used for programs expressly designed by you and the counselors, or to direct students on individual Internet searches following a program on a related topic, college and career sites can introduce students to their next stage of education or their dream career. Many college sites include online applications and information about scholarships and financial aid. Career sites often include hiring policies, job trends, and job interview tips. (Also see the universities and colleges Web sites under "Institutions" in this chapter.)

The College Board
http://www.collegeboard.org/

With "100 years of connecting students to colleges," the College Board has developed this site offering extensive and varied information, including college applications, financial aid, SAT preparation and registration, and exploration of career options. The site organizes the information into logical categories related to college preparation: Plan, Test, Explore, Apply, and Pay.

Future Scan Magazine
http://www.futurescan.com/

This interactive guide is designed especially for teens. The site provides links to the "best career sites on the World Wide Web" while also offering articles and interviews about specific careers. Users can visit the bookstore or the "Guidance Guru."

Internet Public Library—Career and College
http://www.ipl.org/teen/

Visitors to the Internet Public Library can find career and college information in the teen section, which offers links to "Applying for Jobs," "Financial Aid," "Guides to Careers," "Guides to Colleges and Universities," and "Test Preparation." The site also lists a variety of general resource links such as the *Princeton Review Online* and *College and Career Guide for Deaf Students.*

IPEDS College Opportunities On-Line
http://www.nces.ed.gov/ipeds/cool/

The National Center for Education Statistics in the U.S. Department of Education developed this Web site "to help college students, future students, and their parents understand the differences between colleges and how much it costs to attend college." The site allows users to search for colleges based on specific criteria such as geographic region, enrollment, and instructional programs.

Mapping Your Future
http://www.mapping-your-future.org/

This Federal Family Education Loan Program (FFELP) site provides information to plan a career, choose a school, and pay for the education. Users can take "Guided Tours" and learn of steps to take at every grade level to plan for the future.

Peterson's
http://www.petersons.com/

This information-packed site brings together, at one central address, information about educational opportunities at all levels. It also gives individuals the opportunity to search Peterson's databases as well as to request more information and apply to a school or program. Each college, university, and private school has its own site at petersons.com.

Think College
http://www.ed.gov/thinkcollege

This U.S. Department of Education site promotes "Learn for a Lifetime!" It presents information about educational opportunities beyond high school to three different audiences: "Think College Early" for middle school students, teachers, and parents; "High School and Beyond" for high school and college students; and "Returning to School" for adult learners. Besides offering excellent information about colleges, financial aid, and career exploration, the site also includes "Think College? Me? Now?", an interactive handbook for middle school students.

General Interest

A few general sites worth exploring are listed below. They support programs on teen interests, cross-curricular topics, and recreation and fun.

Cool School: The Best Sites on the Web for Teens and Teachers
http://www.coolschool.edu/

Vassar College developed this site devoted to teens and their teachers. Users can explore subject-specific areas such as art, music, physics, or literature, or "hang out" with information on entertainment, sports, magazines, and more. The site also includes college information, with a college search, SAT preparation, and even links to college and university home pages. Teachers can visit the "Teacher's Lounge" to check out both general and subject-specific resources.

Internet Public Library Teen Division
http://www.ipl.org/teen/

Using teen advisors and librarians, this Internet Public Library site offers a variety of links for the teen user. Topics include arts and entertainment, clubs and organizations, dating, health, and sports. Each of these sections includes general resource links with a brief description of the site and the topics covered.

Teen Hoopla: An Internet Guide for Teens
http://www.ala.org/teenhoopla/

The Young Adult Library Services Association of ALA created this site to share information of teen interest. Users can check out the book reviews written by teens, for teens; explore the "Say What" area where teens can participate in forums such as dress code, teen driving, and violence; or search the links to other teen sites.

Newspapers and Periodicals

Many resources on your periodical shelves have Web sites that include much more information and diversity than students can find in hard copy. Some of the most helpful for programming follow:

> *National Geographic,* http://www.nationalgeographic.com/
>
> *New York Times,* http://www.nytimes.com/learning
>
> *Newsweek,* http://school.newsweek.com/
>
> *Rolling Stone,* http://www.rollingstone.com/
>
> *Seventeen,* http://www.seventeen.com/
>
> *Sports Illustrated,* http://sportsillustrated.cnn.com/
>
> *Time,* http://www.time.com/
>
> *U.S. News and World Report,* http://www.usnews.com/

Sports

School-sponsored sports, Olympic competitions, and other popular pastimes are covered in this section. Some sites give general information about the sport and its most prominent athletes. Others give up-to-the-minute scores and headlines news.

*Yahooligans
http://www.yahooligans.com/Sports_and_Recreation/

A sample of the sites linked to this address are listed below. We selected the following sites based on teen appeal.

Major League Baseball
http://www.majorleaguebaseball.com/

Baseball news, special features, statistics, standings, schedules, and information about players all appear at this popular site. While here, visitors may want to listen to a live game on audio or view one on video.

NASCAR
http://www.nascar.com/

This site provides news, race results, schedules, standings, and team information about NASCAR. Visitors can also browse the online store.

National Archery Association
http://www.usarchery.org/

This site, developed by the National Governing Body for U.S. Olympic Archery, provides a calendar of events and programs for how to train for the sport and qualify for competitions.

National Basketball Association
http://www.nba.com/

News releases, special features, statistics, team schedules, and the NBA store are available online. Students will also enjoy viewing information about the players and the history of basketball.

National Football League
http://www.nfl.com/

This popular site contains news, statistics, and team standings as well as information about the players. The special area designed for kids and teens offers football facts, games, and interesting activities. The "QB Club" and "Coaches Club" allow visitors to chat online with quarterbacks and coaches.

U. S. Figure Skating
http://www.usfsa.org/

Visit this site for news and information about figure skating events, athletes, and contest results. Links make up the bulk of this site. "Clubs" lists USFSA clubs around the United States, and "Synch" focuses on synchronized team skating.

U.S. Soccer
>   http://www.us-soccer.com/
>   This official Web site of the U.S. Soccer Federation contains sections on media, publications, national teams, members, coaching, and referees.

Resources to Support Media Specialists and Teachers

Resources that support programming for professionals can be accessed at many of the Web sites throughout this chapter. Here, we specifically list sites that are either exceptional for various educational disciplines, or of particular interest to teachers in individual subject areas.

Copyright

Because school library media specialists are constantly asked about and often made responsible for copyright information, we have created a special section to offer support in that area. Although you probably have considerable knowledge about copyright in general, with every new medium comes another set of standards that we all must follow. We hope that these sites answer some of your questions.

Copyright and Fair Use
>   http://fairuse.stanford.edu/
>   Stanford University Libraries developed this site devoted to information about copyright and fair use. The site is organized into the following categories: "Primary Materials"; "Current Legislation, Cases, and Issues"; "Resources on the Internet"; and "Overview of Copyright Law."

Copyright and Intellectual Property
>   http://www.ala.org/work/copyright.html
>   This ALA site offers a link to the Association of College and Research Libraries, where users can find information and links on copyright protection, fair use, and intellectual property.

Copyright Crash Course
>   http://www.utsystem.edu/OGC/IntellectualProperty/cprtindx.htm
>   Although the University of Texas Administration Office of General Counsel developed this crash course in copyright information for its faculty, other users can benefit from the information. The section that discusses fair use is organized, is easy to understand, and offers "tests" to check for adherence to fair use.

Copyright: Frequently Asked Questions
>   http://web.mit.edu/cwis/copyright/faq.html
>   The MIT Copyright Working Group developed this site, which answers 16 frequently asked questions about copyright, including, "What is fair use?" and "Can I copy films and videos?" The answers are straightforward and easy to understand.

The Copyright Website
http://www.benedict.com/

In addition to looking at copyright as applied to visual, audio, and digital arts, this site offers a section called "The Basics," which outlines information on fair use, public domain, copyright registration and forms, and copyright protection.

U. S. Copyright Office
http://lcweb.loc.gov/copyright/

General information, publications, legislation, records, announcements, and links make up this site from the Library of Congress. Users can learn copyright basics and registration procedures as well as find all necessary forms.

Curriculum

Of all program themes you cover, you are most likely to create programs that support the curriculum. Although you may be familiar with general educational Web sites and those directed to library media specialists, you may be surprised to discover many sites that support various areas of the curriculum. Addresses for some of the best sites are listed here.

ArtsEdge
http://artsedge.kennedy-center.org/

The John F. Kennedy Center for the Performing Arts and the National Endowment for the Arts established this site to help "educators to teach in, through, and about the arts." The site is organized into "NewsBreak," "Teaching Materials," and "Professional Resources." Under "Teaching Materials" users can find lessons, activities, and links, as well as a publishing area and idea exchange. The lessons and activities can be viewed by subjects such as foreign language, science, and the arts, or by grade levels. The lesson plans are well organized and easy to implement.

Edsitement
http://edsitement.neh.gov/

The National Endowment for the Humanities developed this "best of the humanities on the web" and includes the subject areas of literature and language arts, foreign language, art and culture, and history and social studies. Each area is organized by grade level. The site also includes Web sites, lesson plans, references, and teachers' resources.

Health Teacher
http://www.healthteacher.com/

This site "provides a comprehensive, sequential K–12 health education curriculum that consists of almost 300 lesson plans that meet National Health Education Standards and provide skills-based assessment methods." The lesson guides are organized by subjects such as alcohol and other drugs, community and environmental health, and injury prevention. These subjects are then divided by grade levels.

K–12 Resources for Music Educators

http://www.isd77.k12.mn.us/resources/staffpages/shirk/k12.music.html

Resources on this site are organized by band, orchestra, vocal, classroom music, and all music teachers. Most listed resources provide a link and a short description of the site. Other areas of this site include "Music Research Resources"; "Biographies, History, and Works of Great Composers"; "MIDI Resources"; and "Music Newsgroups."

P. E. Central

http://pe.central.vt.edu/

This "ultimate web site for Health and Physical Education Teachers" offers a huge variety and quantity of information. Users can find information on assessments, books and music, research, instructional resources, and much more. The site includes a store, a job center, and schedules of upcoming workshops. The "lesson ideas" are organized in 13 categories, including instant activities/warm ups; health; preschool, K–2, 3–5, and middle/high school; lesson plans; and field day ideas.

General Resources

Diverse sites that equally support various program topics deserve a section of their own. Here you will find multifaceted sites, many of which offer several pages of information to support programs. Although general, they offer concrete help in programming. When you explore these sites, plan to do so when you have extended time. Many will offer a great deal, and you will likely want to see it all.

*Awesome Library

http://www.awesomelibrary.org/Library/Reference_and_Periodicals/Librarian_Information/Librarian_Information.html

This site "organizes the Web with 14,000 carefully reviewed resources including the top 5 percent in education," and offers an area just for librarians. Under "Librarian Information," there are more than 90 links to sites of interest to librarians. The sites are organized by discussions, lesson plans, lists, materials, papers, purchase resources, and recommendations. The presented resources include book resources, book reviews, citations, encyclopedias search, associations, clip art, Dewey Decimal information, libraries on the Web, and OCLC. Some of the suggested subtopics are acceptable use policies, library catalogs, citations, and public libraries.

*Eduhound

http://eduhound.com/

T.H.E. Journal sponsors this site of "Everything for Educators K–12." Users first choose a category from the extensive listing that includes administration, library and research, and virtual explorations. The category then lists topics followed by the links. Each link includes a short description and the URL. For example, under "Library and Research—Librarian," there are 33 sites listed, including links to associations, lesson plans, and resource sites.

*ERIC Links

http://ericir.syr.edu/

This ERIC site offers "Library and Information Science Links," "Educational Technology Links," "K–12 Education, Technology and the Internet Links," and other ERIC links. Recommended sites include *ALA's Links to Library Web Resources, Big 6 Information Problem Solving, The Internet Public Library (IPL),* and *Library of Congress.*

*A Guide to Internet Resources (American Association for the Advancement of Science)

http://www.aaas.org/ehr/slic/internet.html

The American Association for the Advancement of Science (AAAS) developed this site as "a starting point for you for finding Internet Resources." This extensive listing, compiled in May 2000, includes a variety of resources for subjects including math, general science, bioscience, health, college and financial aid, career study, software review, and much more. The sites "have been reviewed by scientific organizations; were created by schools, scientists, or other reputable organizations; and/or have won awards for quality." Some of the quality sites listed are *Eisenhower National Clearinghouse for Math and Science Education, The National Civil Rights Museum,* and *National Geographic.*

*Kathy Schrock's Guide for Educators

http://discoveryschool.com/schrockguide/

Kathy Schrock, a former librarian who is now a technology coordinator, designed this site as "a categorized list of sites on the Internet found to be useful for enhancing curriculum and teacher professional growth." The site is organized according to numerous subject areas that may support library programs. This information-packed resource also includes suggestions for training educators to use the Internet.

*Library and Information Science Resources: A Library of Congress Internet Resource Page

http://lcweb.loc.gov/global/library/

The Library of Congress offers an extensive site filled with important links for librarians. Links are organized by "General Resources," "National Libraries (United States and Foreign)," "Library Home Pages," "School Library Resources," "Online Catalogs," "Research and Reference," "Technical Services," "Special Collections," "Professional Organizations," "Library and Information Science Schools," "Professional Journals," "Library Vendors," and "Library Conferences." The "Library Vendor" area uniquely offers links to some of the most popular vendors for media centers.

*Library Spot Librarian's Shelf

http://www.libraryspot.com/librarian.htm

The *Library Spot* site offers a wide variety of resources about libraries and reference. For the school librarian, the best area is the "Librarian's Shelf," with links to the following: "Associations," "General Tools/Resources," "Libraries and the Internet," "Mailing Lists/Newsgroups," "Library Journals," "Acquisitions," and "Cataloging." In the "Libraries & the Internet" area, there are excellent links for library Web managers. The "Y.A. Services" area offers links to *YALSA, The ALAN Review,* and other young adult sites.

LION: An Information Resource for K–12 School Librarians
http://www.libertynet.org/lion/lion.html

As one of the best sites for school librarians, the Librarians Information Online Network (LION) offers extensive information and links on subjects such as library automation, cataloging resources, CD-ROMs, lesson plans, forums, and organizations. "Issues in School Librarianship" offers especially useful links and resources about topics affecting school librarians, including copyright and fair use, programming, scheduling, facilities, and staffing. The site is sponsored by Library Services of the School District of Philadelphia.

LM_NET on the Web
http://ericir.syr.edu/lm_net/

"LM_NET is a discussion group open to school library media specialists worldwide, and to people involved with the school library media field." The discussion group allows library media specialists to ask for information, share ideas, link programs, and network. Users can subscribe to the group and immediately begin to view or use the site.

School Library Resources on the Internet
http://www.iasl-slo.org/

The International Association of School Librarianship (IASL) created this site to "take teacher librarians to the best 'starting points' for Internet exploration." The resource list includes library and school library associations; school library Web sites; and resources for school librarians about information skills, automation, and reading promotion. The site is "necessarily selective" and discusses the selection criteria. The site also offers "Creating a Web Page for Your School Library."

700+ Great Sites: Amazing, Spectacular, Mysterious, Colorful Web Sites for Kids and The Adults Who Care About Them
http://www.ala.org/parentspage/greatsites/

This list of sites compiled by the Children and Technology Committee of the Association for Library Services to Children, a division of the American Library Association, offers links to "Library/School Sites," "Sites for Children," and "Sites for Parents, Caregivers, Teachers, and Others Who Care About Kids," where librarians can find links to associations, online journals, and much more.

Professional Associations

Professional associations provide direct help in planning programs for other school library media specialists and for faculty. In addition, they can support your efforts to create programs for teens related to different professions and especially to encourage their lifelong reading.

AASL: American Association of School Librarians
http://www.ala.org/aasl/

National standards and guidelines, professional and Internet resources, news about hot topics, and a list of related organizations with links can be found at this site. Also available is a helpful directory with links to state library Web sites, the Library of Congress, and state and regional affiliated organizations of library media specialists.

AECT: Association for Educational Communications and Technology
http://www.aect.org/

"The mission of the Association for Educational Communications and Technology is to provide leadership in educational communications and technology by linking professionals holding a common interest in the use of educational technology and its application to the learning process." The site offers a link to the association's online journal, *Educational Technology Research & Development.*

ALAN: The Assembly on Literature for Adolescents of the National Council of the Teachers of English
http://engfac.byu.edu/resources/alan

This special interest group of The National Council of the Teachers of English developed this site for those "who are particularly interested in the area of young adult literature." The association's journal, *The ALAN Review,* is offered online from this site, as is information about the ALAN Award for "an outstanding individual in the field of adolescent literature." The site also offers links to other young adult literature resources.

International Reading Association
http://www.reading.org/

"The International Reading Association seeks to promote high levels of literacy for all by improving the quality of reading instruction through studying the reading process and teaching techniques; serving as a clearinghouse for the dissemination of reading research through conferences, journals, and other publications; and actively encouraging the lifetime reading habit." The association's site offers association and membership information, news and research articles, conference and project information, literacy links, and publications. The "Choices Booklists" area includes the "Young Adults' Choices for 2000" as published in the *Journal of Adolescent and Adult Literacy,* an IRA publication.

NASSP: National Association of Secondary School Principals
http://www.nassp.org/

This national organization serves educational leaders in middle level schools and high schools. Goals for the organization, membership information, a calendar of events, and hot topics and issues in education can be found at this site.

NCTE: National Council of Teachers of English
http://www.ncte.org/

In addition to membership information and organization news, this Web site includes links to *English Journal* and other resources for teachers. It also provides a "Practical Teaching Ideas" section that offers current teachers' suggestions about literature, reading, journalism, and writing.

NCTM: National Council of Teachers of Mathematics
http://www.nctm.org/

The National Council of Teachers of Mathematics, "dedicated to the highest-quality mathematics education for all students," developed this site to support mathematics education. Users can find the typical association information (membership, conferences/events, publications/products, etc.) and "News & Hot Topics." The "Teachers Corner" offers "Professional Development Opportunities," "Web Resources," "Teaching Resources," and "Activities for Your Classroom."

NSTA: National Science Teachers Association
http://www.nsta.org/

"Promoting excellence and innovation in science teaching and learning for all," this National Science Teachers Association site offers a great "Online Resources" area. Here, users can find all the NSTA journals online, science suppliers and programs, National Science Education Standards, an extensive listing of recommended Web sites, and other professional resources. Under "NSTA Recommends" are "popular reviews of the science-teaching materials that were previously only available in print." Reviewed titles can be searched by title/key word, author's name, grade, category, and subject. The reviews give the material's bibliographic information and a two- to three-paragraph review.

SocialStudies.org
http://www.ncss.org/

This site, developed by the National Council for Social Studies, helps to support the association's mission "to provide leadership, service, and support for all social studies educators." As with the other association sites, information is provided about the association, its membership, news, legislation, position statements, and state and local councils. The site offers a "Teaching Resources" area "categorized by the ten themes of the Curriculum Standards for Social Studies." "Notable Social Studies Trade Books for Young People" are listed in an easy to print bibliography format. Another area to note is the "Media Watch," which lists television and radio programs that support social studies themes.

Young Adult Library Services Association
http://www.ala.org/yalsa/

The sites states, "The goal of the Young Adult Services Division is to advocate, promote and strengthen service to young adults as part of the continuum of total library service." This division of the American Library Association offers resources dedicated to the young adult reader. The site includes information about the association itself as well as membership, professional resources, young adult sites, state and local news, and conference and event schedules. There are also areas for "Awards & Special Projects" and "Winning Titles."

Professional Journals

These resources, both in hard copy and online, are probably familiar to you. However, we thought they deserved to be listed here to remind all school library media specialists that a gold mine for programming exists at every site.

Booklist, http://www.ala.org/booklist/

The Horn Book, http://www.hbook.com/

School Library Journal, http://slj.reviewsnews.com/

Teacher Librarian: The Journal for School Library Professionals, http://www.teacherlibrarian.com/

Conclusion

As you begin your Web searches, you will probably find more information than you can process all at once. Keep in mind our previous suggestion: Start with the familiar and expand from there. Check out some of your favorite sites, then gradually link to others that might directly address your program topic or theme. Eventually, your few favorite sites will become many outstanding resource possibilities.

Chapter 7

Extending, Evaluating, and Assessing Library Media Programs

Throughout the program, "The Hero in You," my guest speakers directly aligned their speeches with the program's inspirational tone. The superintendent was her usual ebullient self, offering a perfect blend of high-ranking integrity and identifiable warmth. Manuel, a former student, aspiring writer, and South American refugee who literally ran with his family across the border to escape his home country, not only shared heartfelt details about the escape that killed his mother but also read excerpts from a screenplay in progress that transformed his own story into a third-person drama. Perhaps most inspiring of all was another former student who shared his story of personal success. When he was a senior, the Tejano band he formed and sang with most evenings was his family's sole source of income. That year, his mother, young brother, and he lived on $6,000. After graduation, he went to Nashville to become a singer, was hired as an agent instead, and now represents many country singers that the program audience knew and loved. Most flattering of all, he explained that he used some of the goal-setting techniques I had taught in the classroom to achieve his success.

These speeches paved the way for my concluding segment, where I shared the idea of discovering the hero inside that could help every student achieve as much success as these guest speakers had. The final activity required students to write on an index card their name and a personal trait that they thought would enable them to succeed. Students wrote descriptions such as self-motivated, strong, smart, funny, concerned for others, deep faith. By the end of the program, many left seeming to be genuinely inspired.

Informal reflections after the program let me bask in its success only temporarily. As a professional, I knew that more work was still required to complete the program process. I had to offer follow-up learning activities for students, express my thanks to all participants and contributors, and do a detailed assessment to determine how effective my program really was.

No matter how successful the event, all good programs must include some type of follow-up activity to solidify or extend learning. As an alternative, you may choose to make a special display or teach an extension lesson before school, after school, or during lunch.

Another essential step that cannot be overemphasized is expressing gratitude to everyone who helped create the program. Whether formally or informally, thank guest speakers, volunteers, and colleagues who contributed materials or ideas.

To complete the final step of programming, conduct formal evaluations to assess your program's merits and weaknesses. Although any assignments following the actual event may seem anticlimactic, they are relevant and necessary for teaching students, for acknowledging guests and volunteers, and for enabling you to improve subsequent programs.

Extending the Program

Even if your program met every objective, student learning can continue after the big event through follow-up activities. At the very least, extending a program reinforces the information shared. At best, it allows students to explore a topic more thoroughly.

Activities for Students in the School Library Media Center

During the planning stage, consider some good follow-up activities to share after the program. Depending on the complexity of the program, these activities may require various amounts of time. For example, one multicultural program featured a display titled "A Worldwide Wardrobe" that included sketches of different ethnic dress. In the follow-up activity for this display, the media specialist invited the geography/social studies teacher to explain why certain types of dress developed because of regional climate (parkas versus saris, for example) and because of cultural beliefs (piercings, veils).

Rather than offering follow-up lessons, some media specialists use interest centers as a means of extending a program. Instead of the "Worldwide Wardrobe" extension lesson, the library media specialist could have created an interest center with articles of clothing from various cultures, maps indicating climate differences, photographs of people from different groups wearing unique garb, and reading material and questions that allowed for independent learning.

Following a program, book displays and bulletin boards make great extended activities in your library media center. Promoting books on your program topic effectively extends learning. Typically, book circulation increases for titles related to your program topic. Sometimes books placed on display are checked out immediately.

After "The Hero in You," I sent each participating student a note that read, "Dear (student's name), I admire your (whatever quality he or she wrote on the card). It is helping you this very moment to achieve your goals and make a difference in this world."

Although this last step may sound arduous, it really wasn't. I formatted each note so that I only had to type in the student's name and the one trait. After printing them all out, I simply folded them in half, wrote the names on the outside, stapled each note, and delivered class sets to the teachers. With very little effort, I added a personal touch that gave students a motivating tool that they could keep and use as needed.

As my follow-up lesson to "The Hero in You," I offered an after school mini-lesson on goal setting. I outlined eight steps for formulating and achieving goals, then encouraged students to apprise me of their successes or check with me if they experienced any setbacks.

Activities for Students in the Classroom

Encourage teachers to develop follow-up activities in the classroom. As support, provide them with a bibliography of trade books, reference resources, and Web site addresses related to the subject. If you have a district professional library, order related materials and inform teachers that you have them on reserve for their use.

Some media specialists carry this support a step further by recommending classroom activities. Like extension work that you offer in the media center, follow-up activities for the classroom may include program-related learning centers, games, worksheets, art, and writing assignments. Whatever classroom activities teachers develop following your program, ask for a copy of the activity and keep it in your program file.

Photo 7.1. Menchville High School media specialist Patricia Scheiderer brings her program to the classroom with a demonstration on reading aloud to children.

Completing the Process

Follow-up activities complete the teaching component of your program. But your work is done only after you tend to a few significant details. One involves a simple courtesy that can have a tremendous impact on your program participants. The others bring closure to your program, while enabling you to determine how well you met your learning objectives.

Thank Your Resource People

The power of gratitude cannot be overemphasized. More than any other interaction with program participants and volunteers, acknowledging their work and efforts will have a long-lasting and far-reaching effect. Therefore, immediately following the special event, express your appreciation to the resource people and/or companies that participated in the program.

Regardless of the ease or difficulty of the program, acknowledge the speakers or businesses. You can thank them in several ways. For some guests, sending a handwritten thank-you note is appropriate. To speakers representing a company or business, send a formal thank-you, typed on letterhead stationery. Also ask speakers if they would like you to send a letter to the business they represented. It would seem appropriate to do so in all situations. However, library media specialists have occasionally found themselves in an uncomfortable situation. After sending a letter to the business, they discovered that the speaker had not secured permission to participate in the program on company time. Although such instances are rare, they are worth noting so that all acknowledgments fulfill their positive intent.

In many cases, principals are willing to send thank-you letters to program speakers. A letter from the principal written on school letterhead adds a professional touch that enhances the school's image. Even if your principal agrees to send formal acknowledgments, you should still send thank-you notes to those participants, also.

Some media specialists enjoy presenting certificates or plaques of appreciation instead of notes. Others recognize the presenters and volunteer staff at a luncheon, breakfast, or similar event. No matter how you express thanks, your thoughtfulness will be remembered for a long time and will make volunteers more receptive to future requests for program assistance.

Some of the best thank-yous come from students. Encourage them to develop a lifelong habit of writing thank-you notes. Although students are required to do so in business courses, it is appropriate to reinforce this kind of formal, polite interaction no matter what class they are taking. As an alternative, videotape or audiotape student thank-yous. However it seems most appropriate, acknowledge your resource people.

Thank Your Volunteers

Acknowledge all your volunteer help with a handwritten note, typed letter, or certificate of appreciation. Send thank-yous to teachers, volunteers, parents, ancillary staff, the PTA, and any other people who supported the program. Although honoring volunteers at a special year-end reception is an excellent way to show your appreciation, always express gratitude in some form immediately following your program.

The day after the program, I wrote thank-you notes to the guest speakers and volunteer coordinators who helped me put the program together. To thank my staff, volunteers, students aides, and faculty members who contributed ideas and display items, I hosted a cracker, cheese, and punch reception a few days after the event. As a courtesy, I also invited my principal.

The tone was light and informal. I created a banner simply stating "Thank you, everyone" and made one brief announcement of gratitude to the entire group. As people left, I gave them a certificate of appreciation.

Update the Community Resources File

Even though volunteers will be updating your community resources file at least once a year, also update it after your program. Add new and eliminate outdated information. To update your files:

- Record a brief explanation of how you used the resources for the program.
- Correct, add, or delete information such as fees, contact persons, and supplemental resources.
- Include information on any new features incorporated into the program.
- Write a brief summary of positive and negative responses from students and teachers.
- Add new resources to the file.
- Delete files if necessary.

It is especially important to make notations concerning the community resource people. Beyond their general effectiveness as presenters, note whether their ideas and vocabulary were appropriate to students. Assessing the topic is equally important. Ask yourself questions such as, Did it pique students' interest as much as I had hoped? Was the material appropriate for my audience? Did it provide relevant and dynamic curriculum support? Record your answers in the community resources file and review them before presenting the program again.

Evaluating the Program

Several evaluation tools are available for determining your program's success. Some entail informal observation that you can make during program presentations. Others include formal tools that provide concrete feedback for assessing several elements of your program. By using both forms of evaluation, you can clearly identify your program strengths.

Informal Evaluations

Making informal evaluations comes instinctively to most educators. Students' blatant and subtle nonverbal reactions during programs can indicate weak points in content or presentation. Written feedback from participants also helps you determine how much the program met your learning objectives.

By Library Media Specialist

Before formally evaluating the program, take time after the event to reflect on how well you think it went. Did it meet your original goals? How did the audience react? Did the program hold their interest? What were the strengths? Given the opportunity, what would you do differently? Trust your instincts. Even before asking, you often know how the program went.

By Faculty and Students

Next, consider essential feedback from faculty and students. Their nonverbal cues during the presentation say much. Looks of interest or boredom on their faces during the program are as revealing as their comments. Opinions expressed during conversations, whether enthusiastic or critical, provide more clues for analyzing the success of the completed program and for developing future programs. Some media specialists jot down their observations; others record comments more thoroughly in a journal. Writing down your perceptions and others' observations when they are still fresh can help tremendously as you embark on your next program.

An obvious goal of programming is to interest students in checking out and reading books. Therefore, observing student and faculty visits to the media center can offer some insight. When students and teachers are really excited about a topic, books on the topic circulate and media center use often increases, at least temporarily. Notice also if books on subjects even indirectly related to your program topic begin circulating more. Finally, patrons' interest in browsing book displays and participating in interest center activities related to the program also indicates a successful program.

Teachers' involvement in extended activities following the program reflects a successful program. Not surprisingly, enthusiastic responses to an effective program translate into long-term interest in the topic well after the event has ended. If a teacher extends student learning about your program topic by generating classroom lessons or activities without your having to ask, you know your work inspired that teacher.

You can learn a great deal by observing changes in teachers and students following the program. Aspire to see school-wide enthusiasm for the topic. Seeing teachers use your program as a springboard for their classroom activities is a sure sign of program success. Noticing improved attitudes about the library media center by formerly uninterested students is another. Naturally, seeing students excited about the topic or skill related to the library program, responding to requests for more books on the topic, and helping students find more related resources in the reference section are all strong indicators of the program's impact.

Formal Evaluations

Formal evaluations give even more concrete feedback on program strengths and weaknesses. By using some of the forms and evaluation techniques provided, you can get a clear picture of exactly what participants experienced, felt, and even learned.

By Library Media Specialist

Immediately following the program, use the instrument in Figure 7.1 (which is based on "Figure 3.1, checklist for successful programs") to evaluate its success. With this form, you can determine how facility and support resources, as well as individual speakers, contributed to the overall effectiveness of your program. After you fill out this formal evaluation, analyze the data.

Media Specialist Program Evaluation

Using the five-point Likert scale below, please circle the appropriate response that best describes how effectively the program item was met.

Name of Program _____ **Date of Program** _____

Program Checklist	Ineffective				Effective
Interest of theme	1	2	3	4	5
Accomplished goals	1	2	3	4	5
Resources selected	1	2	3	4	5
Materials selected	1	2	3	4	5
Publicity	1	2	3	4	5
Scheduling process	1	2	3	4	5
Volunteers	1	2	3	4	5
Furniture and room arrangement	1	2	3	4	5
Seating arrangement	1	2	3	4	5
Traffic flow	1	2	3	4	5
Preparation of AV equipment	1	2	3	4	5
Lighting	1	2	3	4	5
Decorations, displays, exhibits	1	2	3	4	5
Guest speaker	1	2	3	4	5
OVERALL PROGRAM	**1**	**2**	**3**	**4**	**5**

Figure 7.1. Sample media specialist program evaluation form.

By Teachers

Formal evaluations by teachers and students are invaluable assessment tools. While the program is still fresh in their memories, ask them to complete simple forms listing clearly stated questions about the program. When developing the evaluation form, consider the following points:

- Seek feedback immediately following the program.
- Design a straightforward instrument that is easy to complete.
- Design an instrument that is easy to tabulate.
- Structure your questions carefully so as to obtain true reactions from respondents.

- Provide for open-ended comments.
- Assure anonymity for anyone completing the form.
- Collect the responses in a timely manner.

It's important to find out how teachers felt about the program as it related to the curriculum and to students' needs. That feedback alone can determine whether you should offer a similar program in the future. Teacher responses also suggest other program needs. Figure 7.2 is a sample evaluation form for teachers.

Opinion Needed

Faculty Program Evaluation
Program Topic: _____
Date of Program: _____

Using the five-point Likert scale below, please circle your response to each statement that best describes the effectiveness of the school library media program.

ITEM	Ineffective				Effective
Program topic met student interests	1	2	3	4	5
Program enriched the curriculum	1	2	3	4	5
Program provided new information	1	2	3	4	5
Speaker spoke at the right level	1	2	3	4	5
Speaker held audience's attention	1	2	3	4	5
OVERALL PROGRAM	**1**	**2**	**3**	**4**	**5**

Would you recommend that we invite this speaker back next year? Why or why not?

_____

_____

What other topics would you suggest for a school library media program?

_____

_____

List the strengths of the program.

_____

_____

Describe the weaknesses of the program.

_____

_____

Figure 7.2. Sample faculty program evaluation form.

By Students

To get the best input, have students fill out an evaluation form as soon after the program as possible. You may design your own form or use the sample form in Figure 7.3.

Wanted!
Your Opinion About The Guest Speaker

I enjoyed the speaker's presentation.   **Yes** _____ **No** _____

I learned new and useful information
    about the topic from this program.   **Yes** _____ **No** _____

I could hear the speaker well.   **Yes** _____ **No** _____

I could easily see the speaker and the
    material s/he showed.   Yes _____ No _____

I want to find out more information about
    this topic.   **Yes** _____ **No** _____

I read at least one book on the topic before
    the program.   **Yes** _____ **No** _____

I want to read a book about the topic soon.   **Yes** _____ **No** _____

I would like to attend another special program
    in the school library media center.   **Yes** _____ **No** _____

I thought the program was too long.   **Yes** _____ **No** _____

I thought the program was too short.   **Yes** _____ **No** _____

The best aspect of the program was:
_____
_____

The least appealing or effective part of the program was:
_____
_____

I would like the school library media center to sponsor a program about (consider major subject areas, electives, and even personal interests):
_____
_____

Please return this form to the suggestion box
in the school library media center.

Figure 7.3. Sample student program evaluation form.

Circulation Data and Usage

A goal of most programs is to increase book circulation and school library media center usage. Following any program, examine circulation records. Is there a marked increase in books and materials checked out on the program topic? Are both teachers and students checking out the material? The data should provide you with the number of books circulated, types of books circulated, and the populations who checked them out. A significant increase in circulation immediately following a program usually confirms its success.

Examining the number of classes (and grade levels) that visit your media center also gives some indication of program success. Just as important, using circulation data as a program evaluation tool will offer clues as to whether future programs on the topic will garner enthusiastic responses.

Assessing the Program

Once you've accumulated data from students, teachers, and your own records, you can complete your assessment. Sometimes feedback will align perfectly with what you perceived the program's success to be. At other times, you will gain new insights worth having. Best of all, with formal data from several respondents, you can look for consistent patterns that strengthen the value of the feedback. If only a handful of students claim that the guest speaker spoke too fast, was condescending, or was confusing, their opinion may reveal more about them than about the speaker. But if that feedback appears consistently from respondents, it is worth considering.

Examine and Analyze the Data

After collecting and recording the data, examine and analyze it. Keep in mind that not all data are quantifiable. You must take into consideration the qualitative data as well. Look at the reported strengths and weaknesses of the program gleaned from the comments. Your goal for using the data is to answer two questions: (1) Should I consider offering this program again, and (2) If yes, what can be done to make it better the next time.

Informal Data

Consider the informal data that you gathered. Comments, enthusiastic responses, and general use of the library media center may not be easy to measure, but they can still be used to refine future programs.

Formal Data

After recording your informal data, move on to the more formal assessments of your program. Analyzing the feedback that you gather from others and from your own circulation records will give you an accurate idea of how successfully you achieved your original program goals.

Evaluation Forms Data

As soon as students and teachers return their completed evaluations, analyze the data and then use the results to plan future programs. Their input should provide a solid overview of the program's strengths and weaknesses. It should also determine once and for all if you met your goals. Keep in mind that even after the best of programs, you should still compile a list of ways to improve or strengthen future programs on the same topic. Among the data, you will find many suggestions for other topics that interest students and teachers.

The evaluations will also give you some idea of how to improve traffic flow, seating, and general logistical elements that are best determined by trial and error. Most important, use all feedback as an invitation to sharpen your skills and spur further creativity. Do not read constructive suggestions as insults. See them all as helpful tips that will improve future programs.

Circulation Data

Most programs include a goal to increase book circulation. In fact, media specialists occasionally develop programs that focus on a low-circulating area in the collection merely to get the books checked out. Following all programs, examine data for the next several months. Compare circulation for the months before and after the program. Note whether the books in the program category and related categories are being checked out more frequently by students and faculty. Consider the number of materials circulated, the type of user (faculty, student, grade level, subject area), and types of materials (books, magazines, media). Considering all possible angles gives you a clear and accurate picture of your program's impact.

Record Data Results

What do you do with the results once you have them? Begin making use of them immediately. Decide whether to invite the speaker back and record the decision on that person's community resources card. If you want speakers to return, record your own comments about them, as well as any relevant feedback from teachers and students. Include notes about how to improve the program. After collecting so much valuable information through assessment forms, personal notes and statistical data, make the most of it.

Develop a Program Report

Pull together the formal and informal data collected during and after the program. Write a report that specifies the high points and flaws of your program. In addition to being a dynamic tool for you, the report is helpful to the school at large. Share all or portions of the report with your principal, who, if he or she is an effective administrator, will be interested in the data. Information gathered, such as increased circulation following the program (see Figure 7.4) and teachers' requests for specific book orders, will be vivid indicators of your facility's strengths and needs. Your principal will likely include some of your data in reports to the district. Use this information to support budget requests for the library media center or to write grant proposals to fund your collection. As anyone who has written grant proposals knows, most grant requests are fulfilled because of need, not merely desire. What better way to demonstrate need than by including specific data accumulated before and after special programs?

Sharing this information with the principal also offers more personal benefits. Often, the self-assessment of your work will add markedly to your yearly evaluation because your data are concrete indicators that you have mastered the skill of creating effective programs and assessing their educational value.

Program Descriptive Statistics

Number of publicity notices appearing through local media _____

Number of classes invited to participate _____

Number of classes actually participating _____

Number of students participating in the program _____

Number of volunteers _____

Number of requests for additional information on topic _____

Average weekly circulation of entire school prior to the program
(for eight weeks) _____

Average weekly circulation of entire school following the program
(for eight weeks) _____

Miscellaneous notes:

_____

_____

_____

Figure 7.4. Sample form for descriptive statistics.

Your report can include your original program plan, sample evaluation forms, results of the evaluations, comments by students and faculty, and charts and graphs that display the results. With all this information plainly laid out for the principal and school district administration, they become more aware of the demands and rewards of programming.

Conclusion

Programming offers far-reaching and meaningful results. The effects of a successful school library program resonate throughout the school for an extended period of time. Beyond inspiring more enthusiasm for generating work, programs offer students long-term learning benefits. Programs are special events shared through a unique context. Consequently, students often remember what they learned from a program far more than they would during a typical school day.

In many cases, a dynamic program also inspires faculty. Fresh ideas and original approaches can rejuvenate teachers. Your innovation and hard work earn you deeper respect from administrators. Sometimes, one extraordinary event can shift the climate of your entire school.

The benefits branch out even farther. Programs draw together members of the community. Parents interact with business representatives. Companies contributing resources add richly to the overall impact made on teens. Volunteers from outside the school can view the faculty, school, and even education in a better light. Publicity generated by programs enhances the reputation of the school. Even groups who do not participate in the event hear about its impact from students, friends, and co-workers.

Unquestionably, the power of programming is dynamic and extensive. Although much credit will rightly be given to the teachers and volunteers without whom your program could not occur, the real honor is yours. Personally and professionally, the rewards you will reap from successful programming will always exceed your greatest expectations.

Chapter 8

Dynamic Model Library Programs and Ideas

In our discussions with media specialists, many expressed concern about finding time and creative energy to develop original programs. In response, we selected 20 library media specialists from across the United States who shared clear, well-developed model programs and ideas that have already proved successful. Many of these media specialists work at exemplary campuses designated by the U. S. Department of Education as Blue Ribbon Schools for the year 1999–2000. Some have received prestigious awards, which are listed with their name and district location. Some serve on library boards. Others are former presidents of their state or district school library associations. All have received high recommendations from their district school library directors.

Most important, every contributing media specialist has been recognized for exceptional programming. In addition to listing these outstanding professionals and their credentials in this chapter, we include their names with each program idea they contributed. When no single source appears, the program tip is a culmination of similar ideas submitted by three or more media specialists.

In some cases, the media specialist has created an entirely original program. Others use a common format and program type and transform it into a riveting, often unforgettable program. This chapter highlights more than 50 model programs and ideas. Some are original programs described in-depth; others offer clever twists to familiar ideas. Feel free to use the program suggestions exactly as they appear or modify them to fit your particular needs. You may even want to design your own program by combining different ideas. In any case, let each contribution inspire you to develop your own programs.

The model programs and ideas are divided into three sections:

1. Programs for Students
    *   Curriculum: English/Language Arts
    *   Curriculum: Beyond English/Language Arts
    *   Personal Interests
2. Programs for Teachers
3. Programs for the Community

Contributors of Model School Library Programs and Ideas

Marge Cargo
Troy High School
1999–2000 Blue Ribbon School
Fullerton, California
Fullerton Joint Union High School District

Anne Fitzgerald Clancy
Clear Lake High School
Houston, Texas
Clear Creek Independent School District

Karen Couch
Southside High School
1999–2000 Blue Ribbon School
Fort Smith, Arkansas
Fort Smith Public Schools

Karen B. Gaddis
Daviess County High School
1999–2000 Blue Ribbon School
Owensboro, Kentucky
Daviess County School District

Heidi Graham
New Smyrna Beach High School
1999–2000 Blue Ribbon School
New Smyrna, Florida
Volusia County Schools
Crystal Apple Teacher of the Quarter, presented by the
        Southeast Volusia Chamber of Commerce
Volusia Association for Media in Education, President

Nancy C. Griese
T. L. Hanna High School
1999–2000 Blue Ribbon School
Anderson, South Carolina
Anderson School District Five
Piedmont Library Association, President
South Carolina Technical Colleges, Chair of LRC Peer Group

Don W. Hamerly
McNeil High School
1999–2000 Blue Ribbon School
Austin, Texas
Round Rock Independent School District
Teacher of the Year, Excel High School

Amy Hilgeman
Palatine High School
1999–2000 Blue Ribbon School
New American High School
Palatine, Illinois
Township High School District 211
Winnebago Software Progressive Library Award

Cynthia Jones
Memorial Senior High School
Houston, Texas
Spring Branch Independent School District

Jacqulyn M. King
Byron Center High School
1999–2000 Blue Ribbon School
Byron Center, Michigan
Byron Center Public Schools
Regional Media Center 8, Advisory Board
Michigan Association for Media in Education, Conference Committee

Mary C. Mizelle
Menchville High School
1999–2000 Blue Ribbon School
New American High School 2000
Top 100 High Schools, *Newsweek*, Year 2000
Newport News, Virginia
Newport News Public Schools, Virginia

Karen Moss
Memorial Senior High School
Houston, Texas
Spring Branch Independent School District

Mary Oran
Palos Verdes Peninsula High School
1999–2000 Blue Ribbon School
Rolling Hills, California
Palos Verdes Peninsula Unified School District
Golden Apple Award, Palos Verdes Peninsula Unified School District
High School Educator of the Year, Palos Verdes

Liz Sargent
Palatine High School
1999–2000 Blue Ribbon School
New American High School
Palatine, Illinois
Township High School District 211
High School Library Media Association, President

Patricia Scheiderer
Menchville High School
1999–2000 Blue Ribbon School
New American High School 2000
Top 100 High Schools, *Newsweek,* Year 2000
Newport News, Virginia
Newport News Public Schools, Virginia

Sue-Ellen Shaw
New Smyrna Beach High School
1999–2000 Blue Ribbon School
New Smyrna, Florida
Volusia County Schools
Staff of the Quarter Award
New Smyrna Beach High School Teacher of the Year
Volusia Association for Media in Education, President
Edgewater Library Board

Fran Studdard
Clear Lake High School
9th Grade Center
Houston, Texas
Clear Creek Independent School District

Jane Thomas
McNeil High School
1999–2000 Blue Ribbon School
Austin, Texas
Round Rock Independent School District
American Association of School Librarians, Frances Henne Award
Texas Library Association, Young Adult Round Table, Chair

Barbara Weathers
Duchesne Academy
Houston, Texas
American Association of School Librarians, Executive Board
    (representative of the Independent School Section)
American Association of School Librarians: Governance Task Force, chair;
    Long Range Planning, chair; Count on Reading Task Force, chair.
Houston Area Independent School Libraries Network, President
Texas State Library Advisory Committee for School Library Standards Project

Linda B. Wright
Clear Lake High School
Houston, Texas
Clear Creek Independent School District

Programs for Students

Creating programs for students can be particularly challenging. Teens are a tough audience. Beyond their varying educational needs and capabilities, they have diverse interests, attention spans, and expectations for what you can offer them. Whether covering a topic from core curriculum or venturing into topics that address students' personal interests, the following exemplify the best of programs.

Curriculum: English/Language Arts

Library Resources and Skills

Jacqulyn M. King
Byron Center High School
Byron Center, Michigan
Byron Center Public Schools

"Freshmen Orientation of the Library Media Center"

Most high school library media centers offer students, particularly freshmen, some sort of library orientation. The major goal of all library orientations is for students to understand how to locate information using various resources in the high school media center. Special programs developed for orientations vary greatly according to the teaching techniques and creativity of the media specialist and different forms of media used to support the orientation. Jacqulyn King, the media specialist at Byron Center High School, offers several different twists to the orientation program. She has developed mini-workshops for the freshmen orientation that depend heavily on the success of a well-developed mentoring program. She begins by first offering a "Media Center Orientation Mentor Training" program to all College English seniors. The two-day training program focuses on a review of the electronic catalog, the electronic reference databases, and the location of resources throughout the media center. From this group of trained students, Jacqulyn asks for volunteers to serve as mentors. (She is pleased to always get enough volunteers.) She requires the mentors to select and specialize in a specific area of expertise and to prepare and deliver a presentation to small groups. Upon completion of the training session, the mentors are ready to lead mini-workshops and teach students from the freshman English classes about the various resources in the media center.

Jacqulyn begins the freshman orientation by visiting the freshman English classrooms and reviewing information about the media center and its resources. She uses a review game to reinforce learning. For the second part of the orientation, students visit the library media center where they are divided into nine groups and given an assignment sheet that they must complete as they move from area to area (center to center) of the library media center. Freshmen submit assignment sheets to their teachers at the end of the session. A student mentor is stationed at each center and has eight minutes to instruct groups about the particular area. (If all goes as planned, it should take 80 minutes to complete the cycle and introduce each student group to the various areas.) Following are examples drawn from the nine mentors' centers:

Student Mentor #1: Electronic Card Catalog

1. Explain the various forms of media that can be located using the card catalog (books, records, videodiscs, audiotapes, games, filmstrip kits, study prints, computer software, etc.).

2. Demonstrate how to use the catalog.

Student Mentor #2: *ProQuest* Database

1. Show the location.

2. Explain that this is like an electronic *Readers' Guide,* used to find magazine articles.

3. Reveal that articles are available in full text.

4. Demonstrate how it is used.

Student Mentor #5: Reference and Literature CD-ROMs

1. Explain that the media center has a number of CD-ROMs available at the circulation desk (provide handout).

2. Demonstrate how to use them.

Photo 8.1. At Byron Center High School, a senior mentor guides freshmen on a walking tour of the libary media center during a multifaceted orientation.

Student Mentor #9: Walking Tour

1. Explain circulation desk procedures (checkout, overdues, passes).

2. Show magazine and newspaper racks.

3. Guide students through the reference section.

4. Point out the career books section.

5. Explain the professional section.

6. Show the paperback book section.

7. Point out nonfiction section.

8. Highlight the story collection.

9. Let students browse through the fiction section.

Other centers focus on the electric library, periodical indexes, *Infotrac*, *S.I.R.S.*, and the public library Web site.

For the culminating event on the third day, students use the knowledge they have gained during the previous two days to complete a fun-filled scavenger hunt. Students work in their established nine groups, and each team is assigned a table in the library. The procedure is as follows:

- Each team receives a unique list of 20 things to find in the library media center.
- They work as a team and bring each item found back to the team's table.
- After finding every item, each team does a self-check using the rubric (or checklist) in the team's packet.

- After completing the self-check, all members of the team must sit down and raise their hands. The media specialist then checks their part of the rubric. If the team has located all items correctly, the media specialist signs the rubric.
- All students who successfully complete the scavenger hunt receive a coupon from the cafeteria for a free fountain drink.

Through the collaborative efforts of the media specialist, English teachers, and student mentors, the freshmen at Byron Center High School leave the information-packed, three-day freshmen orientation program with excellent background knowledge and skills for using the library media center.

Poetry

Fran Studdard
Clear Lake High School
9th Grade Center
Houston, Texas
Clear Creek Independent School District

"National Poetry Month"

The poetry books in the library media center at Clear Lake High School 9th Grade Center seldom circulated until media specialist Fran Studdard designed activities to excite students and teachers about poetry during National Poetry Month in April. In addition to displaying poetry books, posters from the Academy of American Poets, and original posters created for National Poetry Month, Fran involved the school in several activities.

She asked teachers to submit the titles of their favorite poems. In the beginning Fran anticipated that only the English teachers would be enthusiastic about the idea. To her surprise, she received responses from teachers in all subject areas. (After choosing her own poem, the chairperson of the math department proceeded to select poems she felt would be perfect for other teachers in the building). Fran then photocopied the selected poems, placed them on bright bulletin board paper, and displayed them around the windows on both sides of the media center where they were visible to students walking through the cafeteria and in the English hallway.

She then encouraged students to enter a contest that involved matching teachers' names with the poems each had chosen. Students picked up and returned contest forms to the library media center. The instructions asked the students to match a teacher's name (listed in alphabetical order in the first column) to the title of the poem (listed in random order in the second column). Due to the difficulty of the contest, Fran asked teachers to write clues about their selected poems on their blackboards so students could step into each classroom and make note of the clues. For example, Ms. Johnson selected "The Road Not Taken" by Robert Frost. Her classroom blackboard revealed the following clue concerning her favorite poem: "The poet spoke at the inauguration of John F. Kennedy." The student with the most correct matches won a large pizza.

The teacher for the public speaking classes became involved in National Poetry Month. Each day during the P.A. announcements, she asked a different student to introduce and read a short poem. Students selected their own poems, most of which were already familiar to them. For example, several chose poems by Shel Silverstein, Robert Frost, and

Rudyard Kipling. During the P.A. presentation students provided biographical information on the poet or their reasons for selecting a certain poem.

For future National Poetry Month activities Fran plans to offer a "Limericks or Longer" poetry writing contest in which groups in different homeroom classes will compete against one another. The winning poem or limerick will be published in the school newspaper, and the winning homeroom class will be treated to an ice cream party.

The success of these fun-filled activities became evident in the tremendous increase in circulation of the seldom-circulated poetry books as well as the involvement of teachers in National Poetry Month.

Fran's tips for National Poetry Month activities follow:

- Ask each faculty member for a photograph or take photographs of faculty members interested in sharing the titles of their favorite poems.

- Prepare a bulletin board in the media center that highlights the faculty members and their favorite poems.

- Original posters created for National Poetry Month are part of a kit that can be ordered by going to the Web site for the Academy of American Poets at http://www.poets.org/npm/

- The Academy of American Poets is the largest organization in the United States dedicated to the promotion and appreciation of poetry. The organization also offers lesson plans, E-texts and videos of numerous poems, and biographical and critical overviews of poets and their writing. It can be found at http://www.poets.org/.

- Other useful poetry sites that support the curriculum and library programs are the library Web sites of Kathy Schrock (http://kathyschrock.com) and Peter Milbury (http://dewey.chs.chico.k12.ca.us).

- Fran urges media specialists to publicize the following Web address where students can submit original poetry to Teen Ink: http://teenink.com/Poetry/poetry3.html.

Cynthia Jones and Karen Moss
Memorial Senior High School
Houston, Texas
Spring Branch Independent School District

"Poetry Writing Contests"

Collaborating with English teachers who have assigned students to write poetry, Cynthia and Karen conducted an Internet search to locate sites where the students could enter their poetry in a contest. They provided the teachers and students with a list of poetry contest sites, including the following:

http://www2nypl.org/home/branch/teen/wordsmiths

http://www.writes.org/

Reading and Library Promotions

"ALA Calendar of Events"

The American Library Association has an entire calendar of events to promote libraries and literacy. For complete information about the programs sponsored by ALA, call 800-545-2433 or access ALA's Web site at www.ala.org/events/promoevents. ALA can send you a packet filled with ideas for programs for your school library media center.

Anne Fitzgerald Clancy, Fran Studdard, and Linda B. Wright
Clear Lake High School
Houston, Texas
Clear Creek Independent School District

"Banned Books Week"

Like many high schools, Clear Lake High School participates in Banned Books Week, which is usually the last week of September. The media specialists say that one of their best programs of the year is quite easy to present thanks to the "ALA Banned Books Week Kit," available for purchase through the American Library Association. To order the kit, call ALA at 800-545-2433 or access www.ala.org/bbooks. The kit includes a list of banned books for the year as well as a cumulative list. It also includes the reasons for each challenge and the outcome of the action. Also included in the kit are First Amendment quotations, activities, press information, and suggestions for dealing with censorship. The materials can be used to promote First Amendment rights and to encourage high school students to think about their choices and responsibilities in choosing reading materials.

Displays often include statements from famous citizens about censorship and our right to choose. They also highlight books and authors that have been censored. The media specialists encourage teachers to participate by discussing the First Amendment in their classrooms and having their students read from the banned books list. They also use book and bulletin board displays and buttons to promote the event.

Mary Oran
Palos Verdes Peninsula High School
Rolling Hills, California
Palos Verdes Peninsula Unified School District

"Books of the Week"

The administration at Palos Verdes Peninsula High School publishes a short "Staff Bulletin" every Friday. Media specialist Mary Oran includes a section titled "Books of the Week," where she lists four new books with a brief annotation for each. The books are usually of interest to both staff and students. She always lists one novel and three nonfiction books covering varying content areas so that all teachers feel included. In the first week of every month Mary also describes a unique magazine that the school subscribes to; and during the other weeks she features a Web site of the week, again covering various subject areas.

To further encourage patrons to read about different topics, Mary displays "Books of the Week" near the circulation desk. Although she initially began this project as a way to communicate with staff, students also enjoy the lists, and many teachers post them in their classrooms. She keeps a composite list of all the books mentioned over the months, and occasionally faculty members ask for the cumulative list for summer reading.

Barbara Weathers
Duchesne Academy
Houston, Texas

"Book Day"

Several years ago the faculty at Duchesne Academy agreed to participate with students in Book Day as a community celebration of reading. The faculty also modeled the importance of reading and discussing books as a wonderful way to exchange ideas and expand horizons. The program has just celebrated its third anniversary and shows every indication of becoming a part of the school's traditions.

The first three books selected were *1984* by George Orwell, *A Lesson Before Dying* by Ernest Gaines, and *Fahrenheit 451* by Ray Bradbury. The group did not consciously choose the titles for being controversial; however, because they were the subject of objections to content, the group chose to schedule Book Day during Banned Books Week. In the media center, they set up a display of banned books that are used in the curriculum.

The English department made the selection the first year. The faculty, at large, made the selection the second year. In the future, suggestions will be taken from the students and the final choice will be student-driven. (Preliminary suggestions for the fourth year include the Harry Potter series and J. D. Salinger's *Catcher in the Rye*.) Media specialist Barbara Weathers notes: "It seems clear that we will continue to use Banned Books Week as a vehicle for the discussion."

Barbara recommends the following procedures for establishing a successful Book Day at your school:

1. Choose the book for discussion in early spring.

2. Announce the selection as soon as you have determined it.

3. Add the title to the required summer reading list.

4. Expect all faculty and students to read the work before the following September.

5. Set the date for the discussion.

6. Order the "ALA Banned Books Week Kit" from the American Library Association at 800-545-2433 or www.ala.org/bbooks.

7. Contact ALA if any objections are formally raised against your selected book's content.

8. Encourage students to sign up to be group leaders.

9. Encourage all faculty members (not just those from the English department) to sign up to work with the leaders during a lunch period. Let them decide how to conduct the discussion so that everyone has a chance to participate.

10. At the same time, solicit questions from students.

11. Submit these questions to the faculty committee in charge of the event.

12. Give the same or different questions to each group.

13. Depending on the book, the questions can be scientifically, ethically, or morally driven. They should not be strictly plot-driven, but preferably designed to get the discussion group to "dig deep" and think beyond the superficial.

14. Group students randomly across grade level (20 is a good discussion number) and assign each group a room.

15. During the last 10 minutes of the discussion meeting, give students feedback sheets that request suggestions for improving the event, as well as suggested titles for the next year.

Barbara says, "Our students love Book Day and some have even suggested that we hold the event twice a year. As a faculty, we have seen quiet students come alive in the discussion and talk about issues that matter deeply to them. In addition, the discussions have provided a new way of interacting with our students that allows them to see us more as individuals."

Mary C. Mizelle
Menchville High School
Newport News, Virginia
Newport News Public Schools

"Meet the Faculty and Their Favorite Books"

Students at Menchville High School learn about their teachers' reading interests from a display in the library media center that includes photographs of faculty and staff members holding their favorite books. The idea originated as a special activity to celebrate National Library Week. Advertising by P.A. system, flyers in mailboxes, and word-of-mouth, the creative media specialist urged faculty and staff to become involved in the project and pose for a photo holding a favorite book. They were invited to bring their favorite books from home or to select books from the library collection. Selections varied widely, from one science teacher's selection of *The Dog Care Book* by Sheldon Gerstenfeld to a math teacher's selection of *Math Curse* by Jon Scieszka. *Think and Grow Rich* by Napoleon Hill, *Beach Music* by Pat Conroy, and *Collected Poems of Edna St. Vincent Millay* were among the titles chosen. The selection of favorites sometimes went beyond books. For example, the sailing club sponsor chose *Sailing Magazine*.

Photo 8.2. Students at Menchville High School get to know their teachers through this display featuring faculty and their favorite books.

Using a digital camera, Mary Mizelle took the photographs for the display and made extra copies to present as a gift to each participating faculty and staff member. (The advantage of a digital camera is instant feedback: If the person does not like the picture, Mary retakes it immediately.) She displays the photos on a portable screen so that she can move the display to various locations in the library media center. Following the celebration of National Library Week, she displayed the photos on a bulletin board in the workroom.

Present this display at any time of the year. For example, the display could be particularly helpful in September when students are trying to "put names with faces" of staff and teachers. Based on requests by students, Mary is already planning next year's exhibit of photographs with students holding their favorite books. An additional benefit of the project was an increased interest in using the digital camera in the classroom.

Don W. Hamerly and Jane Thomas
McNeil High School
Austin, Texas
Round Rock Independent School District

"Read and Return Program"

Thanks to combined efforts of the English teachers and media specialists Jane Thomas and Don Hamerly, something unique is happening at McNeil High School. Although Sustained Silent Reading (SSR) programs are frequently used at the elementary level, it is refreshing to find the program in a high school. The large number of books checked out daily make this program a tremendous undertaking. In the first 10 days of school, the program encouraged the 2,300 participating students to check out 1,300 books.

SSR programs aim to create lifelong readers by allowing students to select their own reading materials. English teachers at McNeil High School expect all students to start class by reading a book of their choice, and they quickly become accustomed to beginning class with 15 to 20 minutes of silent reading. They usually read at their desks, although some students prefer the floor. Teachers read during this time as well to model the level of commitment and concentration expected.

The media specialists' support of this program is essential. To keep their shelves replenished with works by popular authors, they must go beyond the traditional ordering from vendors. They purchase best sellers immediately through local bookstores, accept donated books, go to garage sales, and continually fulfill requests by students and teachers. To promote circulation, they offer students book options that appeal to their interests. Seasonal bulletin boards also encourage teen reading.

Photo 8.3. To encourage students to read, media specialists at McNeil High School in Austin, Texas, put a new twist on book circulation by allowing students to borrow books without formal checkout.

The "Read and Return" display in the library media center provides major support to the SSR program, as it welcomes those students who have overdue books or who have forgotten their ID. Students may simply take one of the paperbacks from the display and return it when they desire. Each book in the display has a "Read and Return to McNeil High School Library" sticker on the front. This flexibility of checkout certainly lends itself to encouraging reading, and students never have an excuse for not getting a book. In fact, Jane and Don say that although they keep no records on these books, they seem to always be returned. In fact, some students are more conscientious about returning these books than their overdue ones!

Amy Hilgeman and Liz Sargent
Palatine High School
Palatine, Illinois
Township High School District 211

"Teen Read Week"

Palatine High School media specialists encourage other media professionals to draw upon national reading initiatives and local school programs when developing promotions for their media centers. During the fall 2000 semester, Palatine High School media specialists Amy Hilgeman and Liz Sargent participated in and supported Teen Read Week, an event sponsored by the American Library Association to encourage recreational reading. Amy and Liz added their own unique twists to the program ideas provided by the American Library Association (at http://www.ala.org) by tying their program to Palatine High School's North Central Association reading goals.

To promote the event and encourage leisure reading, they sponsored a raffle in conjunction with the event. First, they created a "Take Time to Read" display for the auditorium showcase that included several new books and the raffle prizes. Then they encouraged students and staff to enter the name of their favorite authors or book titles in the raffle. After the raffle, they compiled a list of the authors' names and book titles entered in the raffle, then posted it on the media center's Web site.

Another activity sponsored by Palatine's library media specialists during "Teen Read Week" focused on Sustained Silent Reading (SSR). Amy and Liz worked with the school's North Central Association Reading Committee members to promote this one-time, all-school reading initiative. Media specialists encouraged staff and students to check out recreational reading materials from the library for this event.

Curriculum Beyond English/Language Arts

Across the Curriculum

Heidi Graham and Sue-Ellen Shaw
New Smyrna Beach High School
New Smyrna, Florida
Volusia County Schools

"Centers for Every Curriculum"

Library media specialists and teachers at New Smyrna Beach High School optimize their lessons through collaboration. Using a learning center format, the two media specialists add a twist. They join with a teacher to review objectives for their lesson and brainstorm ways in which student centers can meet the listed objectives. Then each educator develops two centers or stations, for a total of six different stations per unit.

Over the years, Heidi and Sue-Ellen have designed centers for all levels of freshmen through juniors in history, reading, literature, art, and science. Centers use a variety of media such as computers (Internet, CD-ROMs, and programs such as *HyperStudio*), laserdiscs, videos, audiocassettes, artworks, books, and maps.

After completing the centers, Heidi and Sue-Ellen number each one and write a different sequence on the group folders that students will carry with them on activity days. Depending on class size, they divide students randomly or by classroom teacher into six groups containing four to six students each. Because the class periods at New Smyrna Beach High School last 50 minutes, each unit takes two days, with every station visit completed in 12 minutes. The first five minutes of the first day are used for a brief introduction, and the last five minutes of the second day for a wrap-up.

Periodically, times to visit some centers are doubled. For example, during an Indian unit, a Native American talked with students and taught them a dance. In the Immigration unit, students dressed as one of three ethnic groups and videotaped a narrative on arriving at Ellis Island. Each of these activities required 24 minutes.

At each center, students follow the directions (printed and laminated) and complete an answer sheet or task that is assigned at the station. Because of time constraints, Heidi and Sue-Ellen make directions specific and concise, and they use a timer to keep students on task. After visiting all six stations, students place their finished assignments in the group folder, which the teacher and media specialists check and to which they assign a single group grade.

Examples of Heidi and Sue-Ellen's learning center units follow:

- A unit on immigration uses a laserdisc, a video, posters, a textbook, a camera, and an almanac to write captions for photographs, graph statistics, produce a timeline, and explore life as an immigrant.

- Students explore life in ancient Rome through a teacher-made HyperStudio program and CD-ROMs on the topic. In addition, a laserdisc, a video, and the Internet are used to guide the study of mythology, legendary Pompeii, and the Roman aqueducts and road systems.

- Native American dance, poetry, art, and music are introduced through the Internet, visuals, audiotape recordings, reference books, and a guest speaker.

- American history and literature of the 1920s and 1930s are the focus of one of the centers. Activities include writing a group poem, producing a news broadcast, mapping a road trip, and matching pictures to jazz music. An electronic encyclopedia, paintings, books, laserdiscs, and audio recordings make the various stations come alive.

- A unit on the Oregon Trail has students laying out a wagon (with rope) and packing supplies, writing a poem, mapping a trail, and decoding a message. Various media include laserdiscs, slides, an electronic encyclopedia, and other reference sources.

- The weather unit uses weather maps, the almanac, magazine articles, TV news broadcasts, and the Internet to study weather forecasting and general information about climate.

Nancy C. Griese
T. L. Hanna High School
Anderson, South Carolina
Anderson School District Five

"Displays in the Media Center"

Seniors in all English classes are required to complete a project on researchable topics related to British or world culture, literature, or history. Following a formal research process and using a variety of print and electronic sources, students spend several days in the media center and writing labs researching, gathering sources, and completing the writing process. Finally, each student submits a log/journal and gives an oral presentation describing the special "product" he or she has created to demonstrate mastery of the chosen topic. Exemplary "products" are displayed in the media center throughout the year. Past displays include scale models of the Globe Theatre, pyramids, the Empire State Building, and the *Titanic*.

Family Life

Patricia Scheiderer
Menchville High School
Newport News, Virginia
Newport News Public Schools

"Family Life Students Learn How to Read Aloud to Children"

Family life students at Menchville High School enjoy a unique program in which they learn how to read a picture book to a group of young children. Collaborating with family life teacher Mary Ann Thorpe, media specialist Patricia Scheiderer hosts a special program where she visits the classroom to discuss and demonstrate reading aloud a picture book to young children.

She initiates her discussion with such questions as: How many of you have younger siblings? How many of you have read aloud to them? Which characteristics do children like in stories?

With the previous information in mind, she asks students: What should we consider when choosing a book to read to a group of children? Students suggest various features of stories and books: 1) pictures large enough for all to see, 2) a story that would be appealing to the group, and 3) a story the children could participate in. They also recommend read-aloud techniques, such as the use of props (stuffed animals and puppets) that relate to the story.

Patricia shows the students how to hold the book so that a group of children can see the pictures. Pretending the high school students are young children, Patricia demonstrates the process by reading aloud a children's favorite, *Danny and the Dinosaur* by Sid Hoff. As she reads aloud, she asks questions to elicit comments on the story. Finally, she concludes her lesson by reviewing information that high school students should remember when choosing books and reading aloud to young children. Subsequently, she and the teacher encourage family life students to select a children's book to read aloud to the class. In one case class members chose classic folktales such as *Little Red Riding Hood* and *The Gingerbread Boy* as well as books by Dr. Seuss such as *Green Eggs and Ham*. After the students' presentations, classmates evaluated each other using established criteria, and all students received extra credit for reading a story aloud to the class.

Science

Cynthia Jones and Karen Moss
Memorial Senior High School
Houston, Texas
Spring Branch Independent School District

"Endangered Species: Center and Guest Speaker"

Cynthia and Karen collaborated with science teachers on this program. They invited biology classes to hear a guest expert's presentation on "Endangered Species." To enhance the program, they developed an interest center for students to visit while in the media center. The interest center included a book display, information on the topic, and a bibliography of resources on the subject. (This is just one example of how the media specialist can support the curriculum. Through collaboration with the science teachers, the media specialist can enrich any science topic by inviting guest speakers and establishing interest centers.)

Social Studies

Fran Studdard
Clear Lake High School
9th Grade Center
Houston, Texas
Clear Creek Independent School District

"Multicultural Offerings"

For Fish Camp (two or three weeks before school begins) and Open House, the media specialist at Clear Lake High School's 9th Grade Center produces signs that say "Welcome" or "Welcome, Freshmen" in languages studied or spoken by students on the campus (including Braille and American sign language).

Before the winter holidays, Fran displays signs in the media center that say "Happy New Year" or "Happy Holidays" in as many different languages as possible.

(Fran laminates the signs so she can use them annually. Throughout the year, she stays in touch with the ESL teacher so that she can be informed of new students who speak additional languages.)

Mary Oran
Palos Verdes Peninsula High School
Rolling Hills, California
Palos Verdes Peninsula Unified School District

"United Nations Project"

Each spring, the world history teachers and library media specialist collaborate with the Model United Nations Student Organization at Palos Verdes Peninsula High School. Every teacher has two Model United Nations student leaders who work with the classes on presenting a basic outline of the United Nations and its role and explaining the project. The world history teachers pick two issues (for example, global warming, women's rights, Israeli-Arab conflicts, AIDS, biological weapons, child labor) and assigns students countries to represent.

During this month-long project each class spends a minimum of two days in the school library media center researching their countries and their issues. Mary Oran, the library media specialist, gives a brief presentation and provides a handout outlining the various resources to use for the project, including the latest reference materials, magazines, books, electronic subscriptions, and the Internet. She even makes a Model United Nations (MUN) site available on the library's home page (www.pvpusd.k12.ca.us/pvphs) that connects students to recommended links. She also has a MUN cart with specific books that may not be taken out of the library so that they are readily available to the 700 plus students involved in the project. Mary emphasizes the importance and use of *EBSCO*, *SIRS*, and *EXEGY* for the student research concerning the assigned country and its role in the UN and the world. Students also research and write a two-page position paper on each of the two issues.

Then, in each world history classroom, students participate in a two-day simulation session of the United Nations, with two student leaders acting as Secretary General and Assistant Secretary General. The simulation activity is so successful that many students apply to be a part of the MUN organization.

Ultimately, students will gain in-depth knowledge of international relationships, the UN, and their assigned country and issues. They also learn about new media center resources and become skillful at searching databases and resources for information. The success of this project comes from the library media specialist, teachers, and students all working together to provide interesting and exciting activities to enrich the world history classrooms.

Technology

Nancy C. Griese
T. L. Hanna High School
Anderson, South Carolina
Anderson School District Five

"BBN News Live from the Library"

BBN News, a daily school news broadcasting program, is a production of the journalism and broadcasting class at T. L. Hanna High School. Under the direction of journalism department head, Johna Cochran, and library media specialist, Nancy Griese, students produce, edit, record, and broadcast daily news on a school-wide system provided by Channel One Network. Each morning, two students gather news and announcements sent by the school community and, acting as announcers, record the daily broadcast in a studio located in the library media center. Clips of daily student activities and music are also added to the news program. A variety of editing equipment, including editing VCRs, editing controller, audio/video mixers, and a title maker, is used to complete the production. It usually takes about an hour to completely record the daily news program. *BBN News* is then broadcast to the entire school during the homeroom period.

**Photo 8.4. Students co-anchor their *BBN News* telecast daily for
T. L. Hanna High School in Anderson, South Carolina.**

Throughout the year, *BBN News* features major events and programs, including class and student government officers' election campaign speeches, the introduction of Mister and Miss T. L. Hanna Pageant contestants, science class roller coaster and hot air balloon projects, and "Talks with the Assistant Principal." In addition to *BBN News*, the school uses another program to keep students informed. *BuzzWord*, an electronic news bulletin program presented in *PowerPoint*, is produced directly on the computer. Through the connection of a PC, scan converter, and Channel One Network, *BuzzWord* scrolls all day long on classroom televisions, in the media center, and on a large-screen television in the lunch room. Through this continuous news provider, students and teachers keep up to date with what's going on around the school.

Nancy credits the success of this special program and other library programs to "the complete trust and support from the administration" as well as "the spirit of cooperation displayed throughout the school."

Karen Couch
Southside High School
Fort Smith, Arkansas
Fort Smith Public Schools

"Positive Uses of the Internet for Students"

Karen Couch recommends that media specialists and other educators make use of a fun-filled resource on the Web, *Cybersurfari: A Free, Fun & Safe Internet Treasure Hunt*. She says that students and teachers love the *Cybersurfari* treasure hunts. Through *Cybersurfari* they discover new educational Web sites, use reading and deductive reasoning skills, improve navigation skills, and enjoy the competition of the treasure race. Although food and drinks are not normally allowed in the library, Karen sets up a table for a refreshment or dinner break. (Students love having pizza or tacos from nearby fast food restaurants).

As the contest begins at 3:00 p.m. Eastern time, everyone ready at a computer enters Lycos *Cybersurfari*. Sponsors set up Web sites with clues to follow to find the "treasure." Each clue is presented as a riddle. Students must use reading and thinking skills to decide which link to follow to find the treasure. When students find the treasure code, they enter a key code that has been assigned at the time of registration.

The Web sites are always very interesting and educational. It is easy to get sidetracked on the site, but it doesn't take long to get back on track when another team member yells, "Found another treasure code!" The more treasure codes they find and submit, the more prizes they win. At the end of the contest a list of the sites is added to the teacher Internet book.

Students receive a certificate for level of achievement and a T-shirt. The three schools at each of the elementary, middle, and high school levels that find 100 treasure codes in the shortest amount of time win a cash prize, which must be used for technology. There are also random drawings for prizes. A school does not have to win the race portion of the contest to win a prize. Karen's teams have been victorious three times and have placed in the top three.

Karen urges media specialists to visit www.cybersurfari.org to see what fun awaits them there!

Personal Interests

Artistic endeavors, hobbies, and even unusual pastimes can serve as excellent program concepts. As long as a learning component is present, these programs can be as educational as they are entertaining.

Art

Nancy C. Griese
T. L. Hanna High School
Anderson, South Carolina
Anderson School District Five

"Georgia O'Keeffe and the American Century"

Art teachers and students present annual shows with unique interactive theme projects focusing on the works of various artists. The goals are to combine the efforts of many students and groups into a cooperative effort, to use an interactive approach that will relate the arts to other disciplines, and to involve the total student body in a variety of learning activities. Art shows are open to the public and are held during school hours in the media center in May. The shows are publicized through *BBN News* (see page 149) and the local news media as well as flyers sent out to the community and parents. The most recent show focused on the artwork of Georgia O'Keeffe and other American artists of her generation. Highlights included the following:

- The media specialist constructed large panels displaying students' artwork.
- Guest speakers offered *PowerPoint* presentations about the artists (some based on student projects).

- Students dressed up as Georgia O'Keeffe.
- The broadcasting class filmed interviews with O'Keeffe and showed clips of the art show.
- The media specialist displayed art books (including art history and biographies) related to the artist.

Careers

Karen B. Gaddis
Daviess County High School
Owensboro, Kentucky
Daviess County School District

"Education and Career Center"

Collaboration between the media specialist, Karen Gaddis, and the guidance department at Daviess County High School resulted in the creation of an Education and Career Center (ECC). To construct the center, they moved bookshelves into the area, ordered shelves to complete the layout of the area, and used low shelving to divide the ECC from the rest of the library. Finally, they built counters to support the five computers added to the center.

The guidance department filled the center with numerous catalogs, videos, and viewbooks. The library media specialist updated the collection by e-mail or by phoning toll free numbers and requesting new catalogs from the universities. She also made books available that provide information about how to write resumes and how to conduct yourself during an interview. Karen used the *College Handbook*, which was part of the ECC collection, as a major source for contacting the colleges and universities. To increase material circulation, ECC procedures allow students to check out the catalogs.

In addition to the college catalogs, the ECC offers copies of the set published annually by the College Board, which includes the *College Handbook, Index of Majors and Graduate Degrees*, and *College Costs and Financial Aid Handbook*. The seniors use this material, as do the freshmen personal development students. This class completes a college information sheet and conducts career research during the semester. The students' career searches begin with the *Occupational Outlook Handbook*.

Karen took the vocational guidance books that were already available on a regular shelf in the library, cataloged them according to the subject matter, and placed them in the ECC. Resources such as the following provide information about technical preparation opportunities:

Corwen, Leonard, *College Not Required* (Macmillan, 1995).

Exploring Tech Careers (Ferguson Publishing, 1998).

Farr, J. Michael, *America's Top Jobs for People Without a Four-Year College Degree* (Jist Works, 1999).

From High School to Work: 150 Great Tech Prep Careers (Ferguson Publishing, 1998).

College View (Hobsons) and *Choices 2001* are both available on CD-ROM or the Internet in the Education and Career Center. *College View* is a software program that provides the participant with college information. *Choices 2001* offers an interest checklist, post-secondary information, occupational information, and other useful data. In addition to making these programs available, Karen developed a folder on each college and placed addresses of Web sites concerning financial aid and college sites for schools around the center. She purchased a small television/VCR combination and placed it in the area so students could view informative videos provided by various colleges.

Programs for Faculty

Programs focusing on curriculum, technology, and information retrieval skills can be beneficial to teachers. As well as providing your faculty with helpful information, programs directed to your colleagues promote your school library media center and offer a nice change of pace to programs and daily routines directed to students.

Photo 8.5. In Rolling Hills, California, Palos Verdes Peninsula High School media specialist Mary Oran helps faculty members Karen Yoshihara-Ha, Frank Akins, and John Hangartner "brush up on LMC skills" during a mini-workshop.

Mary Oran
Palos Verdes Peninsula High School
Rolling Hills, California
Palos Verdes Peninsula Unified School District

"Brush Up on Your LMC Skills"

During some inservice days at Palos Verdes Peninsula High School, teachers are given the opportunity to select from a menu of mini-courses, one of which is "Library Media Center."

The mini-workshops are limited to 20 people per session. Mary begins by administering a quiz that tests teachers' knowledge of the library media center. Afterward, she leads a discussion about what they *should* know. Finally, she provides time for teachers to explore the media center, roam the stacks in their subject areas, look at reference materials, browse the magazines and professional journals, examine the professional library resources, and enjoy hands-on experiences with the electronic resources and databases. Under Mary's guidance, teachers particularly enjoy exploring the Internet and the technology lab. Faculty feedback is always positive, with frequent requests for similar opportunities at future inservice sessions.

Mary presents other mini-workshops focusing on specialized topics to specific departments. At these workshops faculty in the various content areas learn about the new books, reference materials, and Web sites related to their particular area. They also learn how to use the electronic subscriptions in that specific area. Mary suggests luring the teachers in with dessert and sharing the current information during a 40-minute presentation that includes handouts.

She offers other professional development workshops related to computer literacy skills in the technology laboratory. There, she gives faculty members plenty of hands-on experience with software such as *PowerPoint*.

Marge Cargo
Troy High School
Fullerton, California
Fullerton Joint Union High School District

"Digital High School Technology Integration Project"

With the state-funded Digital High School Program and Education Technology grant underway, California high schools are required to integrate certain technological skills and resources into and across the curriculum. After applying for and being granted mentor teacher status, Marge sponsored a workshop for ninth-grade social science teachers. She helped teachers design a unit that taught students how to use the spreadsheet program *Excel*. With that knowledge, students created biography timelines for historical persons. During the workshop, teachers learned basic *Excel* skills and became familiar with a variety of library online resources such as *Grolier Multimedia Encyclopedia* and *Discovering World History* (Gale) that would support the unit. The teachers also enjoyed examining the following print reference sources:

> *Dictionary of World Biography,* edited by Frank Magill (Fitzroy Dearborn Publishers, 1998).

> *Great Lives from History,* edited by Frank Magill (Salem Press, 1987, 1989, 1990, 1995).

> *The Timetables of History*, by Bernard Grun (Simon & Schuster, 1991).

As the social science teachers integrated the skills and knowledge to teach the *Excel* timeline lesson, Marge continued to support the project by helping students use print and electronic resources to research their historical figures and the political and cultural events that took place in that person's lifetime.

In the future, Marge plans to offer more technology workshops. Upcoming program topics include Internet search and retrieval, desktop publishing programs, e-mail, word processing, spreadsheets, and *Courseware*.

Karen Couch
Southside High School
Fort Smith, Arkansas
Fort Smith Public Schools

"Focus on Professional Growth: District Planning Meeting"

Library media specialists in Fort Smith Public Schools in Arkansas meet once a month to focus on professional growth. The summer session includes a working lunch when media specialists plan for the coming year. During the meeting, various media specialists sign up to host and develop presentations. Following the session Karen Couch, the leader for the year, finalizes plans and turns them in to the district. The hands-on, interactive workshops focus on a variety of topics and include sample products as well as field trip experiences. Examples of professional development activities follow:

Computer database searches: *FirstSearch, Proquest, EBSCO*

An introduction to *PowerPoint* for the LMS

Periodicals for the schools

Individual *PowerPoint* presentations (librarians present to entire group)

A visit to the new library

Assessment and goals for library media

A visit to Judge Parker Historic Site (Library media specialists will visit the historic site to gain information for the schools to use in Arkansas studies. Using the digital camera, they will develop a short slide presentation for their individual faculties.)

Barbara Weathers
Duchesne Academy
Houston, Texas

"Liaison with a College Library"

Several years ago a college librarian spoke to secondary media specialists at Duchesne Academy about preparing high school students to use college libraries. The presentation was so successful that it led to a partnership between the media specialists and the college. (English teachers may also benefit from attending the presentation.)

The following year the secondary media specialists and the college librarians worked out a system whereby the junior and senior students could use the resources (including electronic) at the college library for one research paper. To be successful, students had to meet specific requirements for information retrieval skills. This need showed media specialists specifically what college freshmen had to know. With that new information, they began collaborating with their faculty to ensure that students mastered those skills.

This program benefits the students, media specialists, teachers, and even the college. Thanks to this program, students have one less adjustment to make when they start college. Also, educators have become more familiar with the skills students need after high school. The college also benefits greatly; it has used the program to write proposals for more staffing and as an example of partnering with other educational institutions. As Barbara emphasizes, "Everyone wins!"

Marge Cargo
Troy High School
Fullerton, California
Fullerton Joint Union High School District

"Professional Growth Luncheons"

To establish a scope and sequence of library/language arts skills throughout the school, Marge and the English department chairperson organized a lunchtime meeting with English teachers. While enjoying the sandwiches and cake that Marge provided, teachers participated in a discussion that focused on the specific skills to be included in the scope and sequence, as related to California Language Arts Standards. During subsequent lunchtime meetings, the group planned research units to introduce or extend skills based on the scope and sequence.

With the success of the luncheon meetings related to scope and sequence, other groups began meeting during lunch to exchange ideas about curriculum. During these meetings teachers shared ideas, strategies, and handouts related to research projects and information literacy skills.

"Teachers as Readers"

Media specialists across the nation have developed a successful professional growth program for teachers based on the International Reading Association's "Teachers as Readers" initiative. The program encourages educators to read books and provides an opportunity for sharing and discussing them. The group should consist of an administrator, teachers, and the media specialist. Beyond that requirement, each group can base further organization on what works best for them. Groups can meet as often as the members desire, and they can meet anywhere: in restaurants, parks, homes, or at school. Some groups meet monthly; others may meet five or six times a year in the school library media center. Consider serving refreshments.

Techniques for approaching this program can vary. Participants can all read the same book, different books by the same author, or different books on a special focus topic. After reading the book, the group members share ideas, thoughts, and feelings as they respond to the literature. Some possible approaches follow:

- The group members read different young adult novels that are new to the library media center. During the session they have short discussions about how the books can be used in the classroom.

- The group members read the same young adult book, and during the session they discuss the work.

- The group focuses on a specific adult novel to read and discuss.

- The group focuses on a specific professional book to read and discuss.

The following tips can help you in establishing this excellent program:

- Purchase multiple copies with book fair proceeds, special budget appropriations through the principal, or grant funds.
- Check with the International Reading Association about grants to defray the cost of books provided to participants.
- Place bookplates in the front of books given to teachers to read. State on the plate that the books were provided by Teachers as Readers.
- Occasionally invite a guest speaker to meet with the group.
- When selecting books for the group to read, consider length, interest of topic, availability, and cost.
- Involve the school principal.

To obtain more detailed information on this program, contact the International Reading Association at 800-336-READ and ask for information about the "Teachers as Readers Group." A video and starter kit are available for a fee.

Karen Couch
Southside High School
Fort Smith, Arkansas
Fort Smith Public Schools

"Technology in the Classroom: How Students Cheat"

Media specialist Karen Couch never dreamed that a simple memo to faculty concerning an article on "student cheating" would lead to a very successful inservice workshop for faculty. *Education Digest* includes a monthly column titled "Caught on the Web" by Carol Isakson. In the March 2000 (vol. 65, no. 7) issue, the column, which offers Web site information for educators, focused on "Student Cheating." After sending a memo and sharing information from the article about student misuse of the Internet for research papers, Karen was approached by several faculty members who asked her to look at some questionable term papers. With a little detective work, she found that three papers were plagiarized. Recognizing teachers' need to know about students plagiarizing from the Web, she developed a workshop on the topic. Using the two resources listed below for content, Karen hosted a 90-minute professional development session to inform teachers about how students use technology to cheat and how teachers can tackle this problem:

Bushweller, Kevin, "Generation of Cheaters," *American School Board Journal* (April 1999).

Keliner, Carolyn, and Mary Lord, "The Cheating Game," *U.S. News & World Report* 127, no. 20 (November 22, 1999).

Karen also developed and shared with the teachers a long list of recommended Internet sites on the topic that discussed the problem and various ways of dealing with it. Two sites that she highly recommends for teachers to use with students when discussing plagiarism are

http://www.indiana.edu/~wts/wts/plagiarism.html, and

http://www.princeton.edu/pr/pub/integrity/pages/plagiarism.html

To conclude the informative workshop, Karen urged teachers to discuss the cheating problem during department meetings and to develop stringent guidelines for outside assignments.

Topic Ideas for Professional Growth Workshops

Media specialists from high schools across the nation provided the following topics that have been implemented successfully in the mini-workshop format. Mini-workshops should focus on one topic, be approximately 20 to 30 minutes long, and involve hands-on activities.

Selection Aids

Many media specialists take for granted their own knowledge of the selection tools that they use to find outstanding books. Surprisingly, many teachers are not aware of these professional resources and are often grateful to learn about the selection aids available in the library media center. In addition to print resources, introduce your faculty to electronic selection aids.

Professional Journals

Introduce the teachers in your school to the professional journals at the high school level. Because so few journals were available at her school, one creative media specialist asked the principal and each teacher in the school to bring a professional journal to the workshop to share with the other faculty members. In addition to the print copies that teachers brought, the group also discussed electronic journals. After the discussion, teachers took time to examine several electronic journals such as the International Reading Association's *Reading Online* and *School Library Journal.* Faculty members left this short session with knowledge concerning the availability of journals beyond their own special areas of expertise.

New Resources in the Media Center

Take advantage of the opportunity to teach faculty how to use new software and equipment available in the media center. Demonstrate and provide time for hands-on activities with a purpose.

Searching the Internet

Any number of topics can be the focus of this mini-workshop. Make it a fun, interesting experience with plenty of hands-on opportunities. For example, the Web sites in Chapter 6 could be the focus of a workshop to familiarize teachers with resources offered on the Internet. Teachers will enjoy sharing these sites with their students. Other workshops could highlight Web sites for the community resources also found in Chapter 6.

Using the Internet for Research

Share a variety of reference sources that can be found on the Internet. Emphasize different search engines. Ask teachers to bring a list of their favorite sites to share, then compile these into a handout for all who attend the session.

Publishers' Catalogs

Several media specialists reported that teachers enjoyed learning about catalogs that we often take for granted. Because we frequently receive duplicates of these catalogs, keep several on hand to give to all attendees as they leave the workshop.

Book Reviewing

This is another bit of knowledge many library media specialists take for granted. Teachers are very interested in hearing about how books are reviewed. Invite a reviewer (university professor or librarian who reviews YA books or professional books for journals) to share information about the review process at a mini-workshop. Also bring in several review journals such as *Booklist* and *School Library Journal* so the teachers can become familiar with the review sources.

Book Fair Materials

Some media specialists arrange for their book fair company to provide a short program for faculty that focuses on the material available at the fair. They usually host this in their media center, giving faculty an opportunity to browse the book fair without students present. Teachers also enjoy hearing about the selection process for the book fair. They welcome a list of the most popular books for children. Some media specialists arrange for the book fair to include professional materials for teachers and parents. During the mini-workshop, highlight professional resources.

Young Adult Book Awards and Notable Lists

You will find background information on these awards at various Web sites (see Chapter 6) as well as in young adult literature textbooks. Select the major awards and notable lists, then give teachers a brief summary of their history and purpose. Make the most recent award-winning YA books available for faculty to enjoy.

Booktalking

English teachers often appreciate programs on the importance of booktalks. At the workshop, share tips on booktalking and familiarize faculty with available resources. One media specialist who offers this mini-program annually commented: "The teachers in my school were excited to learn about the professional books that provide examples of good booktalks."

Bookstores

Invite an owner or a representative of a local bookstore to your school library media center to share information with teachers. For example, at one session a bookstore owner shared with teachers a list of the "Best Selling YA Books of the Year." She also brought along copies and presented booktalks on three of the most popular adult novels.

Paperback Book Exchange

Designate a special week during which faculty bring favorite paperbacks to the media center. Give faculty members a ticket for each donated book. Set up the books on rolling carts in the teachers' lounge. Any faculty member can exchange a ticket for a paperback book.

Luncheons, Receptions, and Breakfasts

Many media specialists across the nation indicated that faculty interest in the media center increased after they attended programs. Brown bag luncheons, economical receptions with punch and cookies, and light breakfasts of rolls and coffee were just a few of the events library media specialists used to spark teachers' interest in the media center. To add a professional development component to the event, showcase new professional and YA books.

Field Trip Experiences

Offer field trips after school to special library-related sites such as the district level professional resources library, a local bookstore, or a nearby university.

What's New in the Media Center

The contributors to this book suggested the following ways to advertise the professional and student resources available in the library media center:

- Make banners and place them on the inside of the faculty restroom stalls. Everyone has to go to the restroom some time during the day, and now you have a captive audience.
- On days that include faculty meetings, display new library materials in the meeting area before or after the meeting. Several media specialists were pleasantly surprised that teachers sometimes arrived early or stayed after to browse through the materials.
- Ask the principal to provide a five-minute period at the beginning of faculty meetings for you to advertise new materials.
- Highlight new materials in a special section of the school or media center newsletter.
- Display new professional materials in the teachers' lounge.
- Use a cart for a rolling display of "New Arrivals" to leave temporarily in the teachers' lounge.
- Develop a creative "New Arrivals" memo and send notes to teachers.
- Display titles of new professional materials on a bulletin board in the teachers' lounge.
- Take the new materials of interest to department meetings and share them with faculty.

Programs for the Community

Programs are among the best ways to involve parents and community members in the media center activities. Consider various approaches. Target some programs solely to parents. Host programs that share information related to students (reference resources for choosing good books) or that focus on them exclusively (Internet search for beginners). Offering programs to them meets their needs and enhances your reputation in the community.

Anne Fitzgerald Clancy, Fran Studdard, and Linda B. Wright
Clear Lake High School
Houston, Texas
Clear Creek Independent School District

"PALS"

PALS (Parents Aware of Library Services) is a library booster club that supports and promotes the library and its programs at Clear Lake High School. The organization's goals include 1) increasing awareness of the needs of the library, 2) increasing funds for the media center, 3) promoting the library to students, and 4) creating an inviting library that fosters learning and lifelong reading. Currently, the PTA solicits parents to participate. The organization also encourages corporate and parent involvement through publicity in the local newspapers. Members and officers of PALS meet in the school library media center after school three times a year to develop and carry out the yearly goals that support the media center. Their work results in book donations and new resources.

Cynthia Jones and Karen Moss
Memorial Senior High School
Houston, Texas
Spring Branch Independent School District

"Thank-You Reception for Elected Officials"

Memorial Senior High School held a special reception to thank some of the elected officials. Among the honorees were state representatives and mayors as well as the school superintendent and chairperson of the school board, who had all worked to pass pro-library legislation in Texas and gain funding for library media centers. Media specialists Cyndie Jones and Karen Moss hosted the event, and the other media specialists throughout the district provided the refreshments; decorated the library in red, white, and blue bunting and banners; and served as greeters. Some gave speeches of appreciation; others invited photographers to take pictures and later publicize them in the school newspapers and on the district's Web site.

A final goal of the reception was to illustrate how the extra funding had helped the district stay on the cutting edge of technology by adding e-books to the collection. Therefore, the district media specialists stationed themselves at various centers to demonstrate how to set up e-book accounts and find and access e-books through the district library Web page.

"Mini-Sessions for Parents"

Programs that directly target parents make excellent media center promotions. Such programs often result in book donations, volunteers, and a bond between parents and media specialists. Encourage parents to visit your media center and become familiar with the role the media center plays in the total school program. Various media specialists we visited recommended the following mini-sessions for increasing the media center's visibility with parents:

- *Media center tour:* Invite parents to attend tours of your school library media center. The tours, which should be informative but casual, give parents an opportunity to know you, become familiar with resources available for students, and learn about library procedures and expectations.

- *Bookstores:* Invite an owner or representative of a local bookstore to your school library media center to share information and titles of good books with parents. With the guest presenter, decide which focus the program will encompass. Popular topics could be award-winning YA books, history and historical fiction, or best-selling adult and YA books from the past year.

- *Web sites for parents:* Plan a parent program around important Web sites describing books and resources for teens. For example, the American Library Association's site offers visitors a wealth of information on resources that can support the children's educational and personal needs. The Web sites for professional organizations listed in Chapter 6 make excellent starting points for this mini-session.

- *Book fair:* On the first day (or evening) of the annual book fair, host a program that allows parents to become familiar with new resources offered at the fair. Usually, the book fair company will send a representative to conduct the program. Provide refreshments and allot some time for parents to browse the book fair offerings.

- *Parents as Readers group:* Several media specialists offer a program for parents that is conducted like the "Teachers as Readers" program discussed previously in this chapter. Refer to that program description (see page 156) for detailed information about establishing the program and ordering the special kit available through the International Reading Association.

Conclusion

There is no end to the program ideas available to us as library media specialists. For any topic, format, or learning objective, there are numerous program possibilities. Clearly, innovation blends perfectly with professional commitment to ignite a spark in you that can revive your school library media center and affect students in ways you may never have considered or thought possible.

References

Albom, Mitch. 1997. *Tuesdays with Morrie.* New York: Bantam.

Ballard, Robert, Rick Archbold, and Ken Marshall. 1999. *Lost liners: From the Titanic to the Andrea Doria.* New York: Hyperion.

Benavidez, Roy Perez. 1995. *Medal of honor: A Vietnam warrior's story.* McLean, VA: Brassey's.

Berger, Pam. 1998. *Internet for active learners: K–12 curriculum strategies.* Chicago: ALA Editions.

Bodart, Joni Richards. 2000. *The world's best thin books: What to read when your book report is due tomorrow, new thinner edition.* Lanham, MD: Scarecrow Press.

Booklist. 1905. Chicago: American Library Association.

Canfield, Jack, Mark Victor Hansen, and Kimberly Kimberger. 1998. *Chicken soup for the teenage soul II.* Deerfield Beach, FL: Health Communications.

Capote, Truman. 1967. *The Thanksgiving visitor.* New York: Random House.

Cervantes, Miguel De Saavedra. 1998. *Don Quixote.* Trans. by Samuel Putnam. New York: Random House.

Covey, Sean. 1998. *The 7 habits of highly effective teens.* New York: Fireside.

Covey, Stephen R. 1990. *The 7 habits of highly effective people.* New York: Fireside.

Defoe, Daniel. 1977. *Robinson Crusoe.* New York: Viking Penguin.

Dickens, Charles. 1997. *A tale of two cities.* New York: Dutton.

Divakaruni, Chitra Banerjee. 1997. *Leaving Yuba City.* New York: Anchor.

Duncan, Lois, ed. 1998. *Trapped! Cages of mind and body.* New York: Simon & Schuster.

Eisner, Will. 2000. *The last knight: An introduction to Don Quixote by Miguel De Cervantes.* New York: Nantier, Beall, Minoustchine.

Evans, Earlene Green, and Muriel Miller Branch. 2000. *3-D displays for libraries, schools and media centers.* Jefferson, NC: McFarland.

Felder, Deborah G. 1996. *The 100 most influential women of all time: A ranking past and present.* New York: Citadel.

Fitzgerald, F. Scott. 1996. *The great Gatsby.* New York: Simon & Schuster.

Gay, Kathlyn, and Martin K. Gay. 1996. *Heroes of conscience: A biographical dictionary.* Santa Barbara, CA: ABC-CLIO.

Geier, Arnold. 1993. *Heroes of the Holocaust.* New York: Berkley.

Golding, William. 1997. *Lord of the flies.* New York: Putnam.

Greenberg, Joanne. 1989. *I never promised you a rose garden.* New York: NAL-Dutton.

Guinness World Records Editors. 2001. *The Guinness book of world records.* New York: Bantam.

Henry, O. 1993. *The gift of the magi.* Illus. by Robert Sauber. Morris Plains, NJ: Unicorn.

It's a wonderful life. 1946. Dir. by Frank Capra. 129 min. Republic Pictures,videocassette.

John-Roger, and Peter McWilliams. 1991. *Do it! Let's get off our buts.* Los Angeles, CA: Prelude.

John-Roger, and Peter McWilliams. 1990. *Life 101.* Los Angeles, CA: Prelude.

Keller, Helen. 1991. *Helen Keller: The story of my life.* New York: Dell.

Lee, Harper. 1999. *To kill a mockingbird.* New York: HarperCollins.

Medoff, Mark. 1994. *Children of a lesser god.* New York: Dramatists Play Service.

Morrison, Toni. 1998. *Beloved.* New York: Dutton.

Paulsen, Gary. 1999. *Hatchet.* New York: Simon & Schuster.

Poe, Edgar Allan. 1999. *The pit and the pendulum and other stories by Edgar Allan Poe.* Illus. by Jame's Prunier. New York: Viking.

Powell, Randy. 1999. *Tribute to another dead rock star.* New York: Farrar, Straus & Giroux.

Ravinovici, Schoschana. 1998. *Thanks to my mother.* New York: Dial Press.

Ryan, Bernard, Jr. 1998a. *Community service for teens: Expanding education & literacy.* Chicago: Ferguson.

Ryan, Bernard, Jr. 1998b. *Community service for teens: Helping the ill, the poor, & the elderly.* Chicago: Ferguson.

Ryan, Bernard, Jr. 1998c. *Community service for teens: Serving with police, fire, & e.m.s.* Chicago: Ferguson.

Scieszka, Jon. 1995. *Math curse.* Illus. by Lane Smith. New York: Viking.

Seuss, Dr. 1990. *Oh, the places you'll go.* New York: Random House.

Solzhenitsyn, Aleksandr Isaevich. 1998. *One day in the life of Ivan Denisovich.* New York: Penguin.

Stone, Irving. 1984. *Lust for life.* New York: Dutton.

Sullivan, Tom, and Derek L. Gill. 1989. *If you could see what I hear.* New York: Harper.

Thatcher, Kevin J. 1992. *Thrasher: The radical skateboard book.* New York: Random House.

Walker, Alice. 1998. *The color purple.* New York: Pocket.

Weisel, Elie. 1982. *Night.* New York: Bantam.

White Squall. 1996. Dir. by Ridley Scott. 128 min. Buena Vista, videocassette.

Whitman, Walt. 1976. *The complete poems.* New York: Penguin.

Wilson, Patricia Potter, and Ann C. Kimzey. 1987. *Happenings: Developing successful programs for school libraries.* Englewood, CO: Libraries Unlimited.

Wilson, Patricia Potter, and Roger Leslie. 2001. *Premiere events: Library programs that inspire elementary school patrons.* Englewood, CO: Libraries Unlimited.

Winfrey, Oprah, and Bob Green. 1999. *Make the connection: Ten steps to a better body and a better life.* Illus. by Julie Johnson. New York: Hyperion.

Your parents aren't supposed to like it. 1998. Detroit: Gale Research. [three-volume set]

Index

About the Authors

Roger Leslie is an author, editor, teacher, library media specialist, and book reviewer with 15 years of experience in public education. Before becoming a school library media specialist, he taught all levels of secondary English and creative writing, served as department chairperson, and coached the Academic Decathlon team as well as several University Interscholastic League groups related to the humanities.

Many of his early writings came directly from his classroom experiences. He has published numerous educational articles in journals throughout the United States, including *English in Texas, California English,* and *North Carolina English Teacher.* His personal essays appear regularly in *Texas Magazine,* and two of his latest efforts are anthologized in *Voices of Michigan, Volume 2* (MackinacJane's, 2000) and *Volume 3* (2001). Leslie is also a book reviewer for the Young Adult section of the American Library Association's *Booklist.*

Leslie's major works include history books, novels, biographies, and screenplays. A specialist in motivation and self-esteem building, he has recently returned to his teaching role by visiting classrooms and sharing concepts from his book, *Train of Dreams: Your Journey to Success and Self-Discovery.* His latest novel, *Drowning in Secret*, will be published by Absey & Company in spring 2002.

As both a writer and a teacher, Leslie has received many honors. A comic one-act play and his first published book, *Galena Park: The Community That Shaped Its Own History* (1993), brought him special recognition and local citizens' awards. He also has received Teacher of the Year awards from such groups as Texas A & M University, The University of Texas, and Houston's North Channel Chamber of Commerce. In 1989, Leslie was Galena Park I.S.D. District Teacher of the Year. He was featured on ABC News's "Teachers Make a Difference" show, listed in *Who's Who Among America's Teachers* (1992–1996), and has been named one of the Outstanding Young Men of America for the past four years.

Dr. Patricia Potter Wilson is an associate professor in the School of Education at University of Houston-Clear Lake, where she teaches children's literature and reference and supervises the internships in the School Library and Information Science Program.

An active member of professional organizations related to school libraries and reading, she is a frequent presenter at national and state conferences such as the American Association of School Librarians, National Council of Teachers of English, and International Reading Association. She was awarded the Texas Council of Teachers of English President's Research Award and the Texas State Reading Association Research Award.

Her major research interest involves the examination of principal-preparation programs at universities to determine the amount of emphasis they place on school library media centers. Based on this research, she is currently designing a school library component that will be placed in the principal-preparation courses.

Dr. Wilson is the author of *The Professional Collection for Elementary Educators* (H. W. Wilson, 1996) and co-author of *Happenings: Developing Successful Programs for School Libraries* (Libraries Unlimited, 1987). She has published numerous articles related to teaching and research in professional journals such as *School Library Journal, Reading Teacher, Journal of Youth Services, Reading Horizons, Teacher Librarian, National Forum of Educational Administration and Supervision Journal, National Forum of Teacher Education Journal,* and *National Forum of Applied Educational Research Journal.*

Among her many honors, she was selected as the 1999 Outstanding Alumna by the University of Houston-Clear Lake Alumni Association. She received the Enron Teaching Excellence Award and the President's Distinguished Teaching Award at University of Houston-Clear Lake in 1996. Dr. Wilson was also selected by students and faculty at University of Houston-Clear Lake as the 1996 Piper Professor Nominee, which honors outstanding professors. Listed in Marquis's *Who's Who in America, Who's Who in American Women,* and *Who's Who in American Education,* Dr. Wilson serves on various library and literacy-related boards in the Houston area.